SELECTED POEMS OF
WILLIAM BLAKE

THE POETRY BOOKSHELF

General Editor: James Reeves

SELECTED POEMS OF

WILLIAM BLAKE

Edited with an Introduction

and Explanatory Notes

by

F. W. BATESON

HEINEMANN

LONDON

Heinemann Educational Books Ltd

LONDON EDINBURGH MELBOURNE AUCKLAND TORONTO
SINGAPORE HONG KONG KUALA LUMPUR
IBADAN NAIROBI JOHANNESBURG
LUSAKA NEW DELHI

WILLIAM BLAKE 1757–1827

ISBN 0 435 15010 3 (cased edition)
ISBN 0 435 15011 1 (paperback)

INTRODUCTION AND NOTES © F. W. BATESON 1957
FIRST PUBLISHED 1957
REPRINTED WITH CORRECTIONS 1961
REPRINTED 1963, 1964, 1965, 1968, 1969, 1971,
1974, 1976

Published by
Heinemann Educational Books Ltd
48 Charles Street, London W1X 8AH
Printed in Great Britain by Morrison and Gibb Ltd
London and Edinburgh

CONTENTS

PREFACE

THE total intelligibility of Blake's poetry is a modern discovery. In *The English Poets* (1880) of Thomas Humphry Ward (of which Matthew Arnold, Ward's brother-in-law, was the inspiring genius) Blake is still the mad poet: 'Blake has been called mad, and within certain well-defined limits the charge must, we think, be admitted.' The admission is made apologetically, with regret. To A. E. Housman, on the other hand, whose eulogy typifies the next stage in the growth of Blake's reputation, it was the madness that made Blake 'the most poetical of all poets'. Because of it, as he explains in *The Name and Nature of Poetry* (1933), Blake 'gives us poetry neat, or adulterated with so little meaning that nothing except poetic emotion is perceived and matters'. A dark saying, but presumably what Housman liked was the fantastic or phantasmagoric quality in Blake's symbolism. But we now know, thanks to a generation of Blake scholarship, most of it trans-Atlantic, that the fantasies Housman admired because they were meaningless function in a completely rational and explicable framework. Blake was not mad but obscure. In the later poetry in particular he was trying to say too many things at the same time, and it is not always clear at which level of meaning the emphasis comes or at what point one level begins and another ends. Because of this still formidable obscurity no editor has been bold enough so far to bring out a selection from Blake with full explanatory notes. But a beginning must be made sometime, and though inadequate in many respects the notes in the present edition can hardly fail to be better than none at all.

It has not seemed necessary to record the sources and authorities for every separate item of information, but I am particularly indebted to the following works: S. Foster Damon, *William Blake, his Philosophy and Symbols* (1924); Mona Wilson, *The Life of William Blake* (1927, revised 1948); Northrop Frye, *Fearful Symmetry, a Study of William Blake* (1947); Geoffrey Keynes and Edwin Wolf, *William Blake's Illuminated Books, a Census* (1953); David V. Erdman, *Blake Prophet against Empire* (1954); Stanley Gardner, *Infinity on the Anvil, a Critical Study of Blake's Poetry* (1954).

The text has been largely normalized, except in the extracts from *An Island in the Moon*. Blake's punctuation is so erratic that its minute preservation would simply create an unnecessary barrier between the reader and Blake's meaning. And if the punctuation is modernized it would be illogical to retain all of Blake's oddities of spelling and capitalisation (which are in any case only occasionally of any interest). Excellent facsimiles can now be obtained of all the poetic works, and the interested reader may be referred to them. Indeed, no one has 'read' Blake unless he has seen at least one example of the superb 'Illuminated Printing' in which most of the poems were originally issued.

F. W. BATESON

Corpus Christi College,
Oxford.

Introduction

WILLIAM BLAKE
(1757-1827)

I

THE London into which William Blake was born on November 28th, 1757, was the object some thirty-five years later of two of his most biting and memorable lines:

> I wander through each chartered street,
> Near where the chartered Thames does flow. . . .

In the poem's first draft the opprobrious epithet had not been 'chartered' but 'dirty' ('dirty street', 'dirty Thames'), but by the time *London* was engraved for *Songs of Experience* the mere physical pollution had come to seem less oppressive to Blake than the spiritual tyranny exercised by the City of London, its boroughs and its incorporated companies. Magna Carta had once been a guarantee of English freedom, but by the eighteenth century the charters, from which not even the Thames was exempt, were empowering a minority of Londoners to impose their 'mind-forged manacles' on the rest of their fellow-citizens. So, at any rate, it seemed, with some justice, to the adult Blake. For the child, naturally, the dirt was that of the dirty street in which he lived—Broad Street, Carnaby Market. (It is only two hundred yards or so to the east of what is now Regent Street.) And the infantile tyrants were his father James Blake, who did a 'respectable trade' as hosier at 28 Broad Street, and his wife Catherine. Except that they were both Dissenters not much is discoverable about Blake's father and mother,[1] but the general pattern of the family's internal relationships can be reconstructed from the anecdotes that have survived of Blake's childhood. It is a story not so much of unkindness as of incomprehension.

According to Frederick Tatham, the young sculptor and miniature painter to whom Blake left his manuscripts, James Blake was 'by his son's description a lenient and affectionate father'. But, if well-meaning, he was essentially a man of 'moderate desires, moderate enjoyments'—the psychological opposite of his explosive, extremist son. The mother is a dim, unsympathetic figure, and there were four other children, William coming second. James, the eldest, is described by Tatham as 'having a saving, somniferous mind', who 'lived a yard and a half life' and pestered William 'with timid sentences of bread and cheese advice'. Tatham, who was no phrase-maker, is probably echoing Blake's own complaints here about the virtuous elder brother; the two were not even on speaking terms towards the end of their lives. The parents' favourite, however, was John, who came next after William, being only a year and a half his junior. Tatham describes him as 'a dissolute, disreputable youth', about whose behaviour 'William often remonstrated, and was as often told to be quiet, and that he would bye and bye beg his bread at John's door'. Nearly sixty years had passed by the time Blake confided these early humiliations to Tatham, but evidently their memory was still rankling. In the end, Blake added triumphantly, it was John who begged bread at William's door, and then 'lived a few reckless days, enlisted as a soldier, and died'.

[1] The fathers and mothers who figure in *Songs of Experience* and the later poems must not be identified with Blake's own father and mother, but it is impossible not to accord them some unconscious autobiographical significance. Here, for example, from the original draft of *A Little Boy Lost*, is a typical mother encouraging a typical priest:

> The mother followed, weeping loud,
> 'Oh that I such a fiend should bear!'

John is mentioned by name only once in Blake's poetry—in the lines beginning, 'With happiness stretched across the hills':

> my brother John, the evil one,
> In a black cloud making his moan.

But John's influence, or rather the influence of the mother's love that was diverted to him and away from the only slightly older William, must be taken into account in any attempt to understand Blake. The deprivation helps to explain his intense, abnormal subjectivity. In unconscious compensation for the understanding and affection denied to him at home he created for himself, as any child might have done in the same situation, an exotic imaginary world of his own. But the exceptional acuteness of his pictorial sense (he drew beautifully even as a boy) made it much more real to him than such fantasy-worlds usually are. And unfortunately the very vividness of Blake's childish daydreams created only another barrier between him and his parents. To the pious hosier and his commonplace wife the long walks that the little William was soon in the habit of taking into the open country—which was still only a mile or two from Carnaby Market—were no doubt suspect in themselves, and the stories that he began to bring back of angels he had seen with his own eyes and Old Testament prophets he had conversed with must have seemed nothing but blasphemous lies, for which the only possible remedy was a sound whipping.

Once, coming back from Dulwich, when he was about seven years old, he told the family that he had seen a tree full of angels, 'their bright wings bespangling the boughs like stars'—a piece of poetry to which Mr. Blake's immediate reaction was to set about thrashing the original sin out of the little liar. On this occasion he was saved by his mother's intervention, but it was she who, according to Tatham, 'beat him for running in and saying that he saw the prophet Ezekiel under a tree in the fields'. The effect of such treatment on a proud and sensitive boy is not difficult to imagine. In addition to driving him into himself more than ever the unfairness of such punishments made him resent them almost to the point of hysteria, so that even his philistine parents could not help getting alarmed. The reason why he never went to school, according to Tatham, was that he 'so hated a blow' that his father was afraid to expose him to the rigours of ordinary school discipline. The brilliance of the early poems and drawings may also, of course, have had something to do with the increasing leniency. Perhaps somebody told the Blakes that the author of a poem like, 'How sweet I roamed from field to field' (which is known to have been written before he was fourteen) was an infant prodigy who must not be treated quite like other children.

A significant feature of the early 'visions'—it is equally true of the early poems—is that their setting is always in the country. The angelic figures that he saw walking, according to another anecdote, in and out among the human haymakers in a suburban hayfield never came to Broad Street. Except on one occasion— when God 'put his head to the window' and frightened the four-year-old Blake into a paroxysm of screams—the scene of the visions was never in the man-made town. It will be remembered that none of Wordsworth's early mystical experiences occurred in Penrith, although nearly half of his childhood was spent in a mercer's shop in that dismal town. In Blake's case an almost complete mental hiatus seems to have developed between the ideal golden world that he created for himself on his solitary country walks and the urban realities of the chartered streets and the drab, puritanical hosiery shop. But with Blake, as with Wordsworth, the division was not simply a case of escapism. It had its roots in reality, the reality of a moral protest against unbearable human conditions, and it is this moral realism that informs the last and perhaps the most potent of Blake's myths— that of rebuilding Jerusalem 'In England's green and pleasant land'. The basis of the myth was unquestionably the memories of 'The fields from Islington to Marylebone', 'The ponds where boys to bathe delight', and 'The fields of cows by Willan's Farm', that are listed so affectionately in the interchapter between the first and second chapters of *Jerusalem*, although by 1820, when *Jerusalem* was completed, the London builders or Regent's Park had long been in possession of them. In Blake's childhood these fields were the beginning of the real country, where it was nearest and most accessible to the inhabitants of Carnaby Market. As he left behind the mud, soot and sweat of Broad Street they may well have seemed to be 'builded over with pillars of gold'. And in less specific form the country around London in which he had walked as a boy is also—there can be no doubt about this—the symbolic setting of the spiritual condition that he called Innocence.

The imagery of Experience, on the other hand, both in the Songs of Experience and in the so-called Prophetic Books that grew out of them, came out of Blake's dreams. The distinction is crucial to an understanding of the symbolic system that underlies all his poems. The fantasy-world of Innocence was essentially a daylight world. In *The Echoing Green* and *Nurse's Song* all the laughing and the shouting stop abruptly as the dark comes. But the geography of Experience—for example, the Tiger's 'forests of the night'—begins *after* the Nurse has put the little ones to bed. And of the terrifying nature of Blake's own infantile dreams there can surely be little doubt. The snakes who writhe in and through and around so many of his paintings and engravings, often for no discoverable reason at all, are obviously the progeny of nightmare. So too is the Neanderthal monster who turns up not only in the powerful and gruesome painting that Blake called 'The Ghost of a Flea', but also as Pestilence in 'Pestilence: the Death of the First-Born', and as Goliath in 'David and Goliath'. The atmosphere of struggle and agony, the 'howlings' (a favourite word of Blake's almost to the point of obsession) and the torments, although sometimes put to good artistic or poetic use, all descend—or so it would seem (there can, of course, be no conclusive evidence in a matter of this kind) —from the bad dreams of an unhappy and unusually imaginative child. If the young Blake found his Heaven in the 'pleasant pastures' on the outskirts of London, there can be little doubt, I think, that his Hell came to him upstairs in bed after the hosiery shop had been shut.

Fortunately Blake's childhood was not confined to Broad Street. There were relations or connections who lived at Battersea and Kew, and the unloved, difficult, original little boy was occasionally bundled off to them. The early poem *Blind Man's Buff*, which describes the high jinks of a young people's party on a country evening in winter, must be the recollection of one such visit. It is a reassuringly sane poem that suggests Henry Carey, the author of *Sally in Our Alley*, rather than an eighteenth-century Gothic novel or Macpherson's Ossianic extravagances. And Tilly Lally the schoolboy, who sings a song in *An Island in the Moon* about an unusual game of cricket, is reassuringly boyish. Several of the songs in that high-spirited satire, which was completed when Blake was just twenty-seven and probably incorporates earlier material, show that, in spite of all the evidence to the contrary, his childhood was not completely cut off from the everyday world of the eighteenth century. Miss Gittipin sings a nursery rhyme ('This frog he would a-wooing ride'), Mrs. Nannicantipot obliges with a London street-cry ('I cry my matches as far as Guildhall'), and Steelyard's 'As I walked forth one May morning' *sounds* like a traditional folk-song, even if it may not be one in fact. Blake was a musical young man, making up his own tunes to the songs he wrote, and he was always prepared to sing them publicly to a sympathetic audience. J. T. Smith, the author of that minor classic *Nollekens and his Times*, who had been a playfellow of Robert Blake's (the youngest of the brothers and William's special favourite), reports that Blake's ear was so good 'that his tunes were sometimes most singularly beautiful, and were noted down by musical professors'. In addition to the early songs some of the Songs of Innocence may also have been set to music by Blake himself. In spite of the 'musical professors', however, none of the tunes have survived. But the wording and metrical structure of the songs make it clear that they must have been in what can be called the folk-song tradition, if that category may be allowed to include street ballads, hymns, metrical versions of the psalms, and such things as Isaac Watts's *Divine and Moral Songs*, as well as folk-songs proper such as those in Thomas Durfey's *Pills to Purge Melancholy*. The point is one of some critical importance. It is precisely the popular, realistic, colloquial tone of the Songs of Innocence and Experience, and the manuscript lyrics associated with them, that differentiates them *toto caelo* from the declamatory rhetoric of the Prophetic Books. The origins of the lyrics are in communal entertainment and communal religion; the Prophetic Books, in so far as they do not come straight out of Blake's head, are the products of a recondite learning and pseudo-learning.

II

A short summary must suffice for the external events in Blake's life. At the age of ten he was sent to a good drawing-school in the Strand, and four years later, in 1772, he began a seven years' apprenticeship in engraving under James Basire. He did well as an engraver in the hard, wiry manner practised by Basire, and when the apprenticeship was completed he found himself with plenty of orders from the booksellers. At this time he also began to attend classes in painting at the Royal Academy. In 1780 he exhibited his first picture—'Death of Earl Godwin' —at the Academy, and he soon made friends with such promising young artists as John Flaxman, Thomas Stothard and Henry Fuseli. Fuseli, a Swiss by birth and an exceptionally cultivated and original man, ultimately became Blake's closest and most loyal friend. In 1782 he married Catherine Boucher or Butcher, a Battersea tradesman's daughter whom he taught to read and to help in the colouring of his engravings.[1] Kate, as he called her, was a beautiful girl, with the graceful attenuated figure so familiar in Blake's paintings and engravings, and she made him an excellent wife. The early poems, including those with which he had wooed her, were printed in 1783 as *Poetical Sketches*. Old Mr. Blake died in 1784, and on the strength of what he had inherited plus some assistance from Mrs. Anthony Stephen Mathew, a kindly bluestocking who took up Blake at this time, he and James Parker (who had been a fellow-apprentice under Basire) set up a print-shop in Broad Street next door to the family hosiery. Robert Blake, who was five years younger than William and the only other member of the family with any artistic talent, joined William and Kate at the print-shop as a pupil-assistant, and an anecdote recorded by Alexander Gilchrist, the author of the first full-length biography of Blake, gives a lively picture of the ménage:

> One day a dispute arose between Robert and Mrs. Blake. She, in the heat of discussion, used words to him his brother (though a husband too) thought unwarrantable. A silent witness thus far, he could now bear it no longer, but with characteristic impetuosity— when stirred—rose and said to her: 'Kneel down and beg Robert's pardon directly, or you never see my face again!' A heavy threat, uttered in tones which, from Blake, unmistakably showed it was *meant*. She, poor thing, 'thought it very hard', as she would after- wards tell, to beg her brother-in-law's pardon when she was not in fault! But being a duteous, devoted wife, though by nature nowise tame or dull of spirit, she *did* kneel down and meekly murmur: '*Robert, I beg your pardon, I am in the wrong.*' 'Young woman, you lie!' abruptly retorted he: '*I am in the wrong.*'

[1] Mrs. Blake's grammar, however, was always a little uncertain. 'You see,' she told George Richmond years later, by way of excusing the general lack of soap and water in the establishment, 'Mr. Blake's skin don't dirt!'

But the print-shop only lasted a year and Robert died of consumption in February 1787—a tragedy to which Blake reacted by the self-deception (a return to the neurotic subjectivity of his childhood) of continuing to live and converse with his brother 'in the regions of my imagination'. After Robert's death (he was twenty-four—some of his drawings have been confused with William's) the Blakes moved round the corner into Poland Street. From this point Blake's external history is largely that of his writings, most of which are discussed separately in the notes to this edition, his paintings and his engravings. The first experiments in 'Illuminated Printing'—the process of relief-etching followed by hand-colouring in which, with minor technical modifications, almost all Blake's later poems were originally published—date from 1788. In 1791 there was a removal to a larger house at Lambeth—just behind an orphanage in the Westminster Bridge Road—from which most of the Prophetic Books were issued. In 1800, through Flaxman's well-meant intervention, the Blakes moved down to Felpham in Sussex, where William Hayley, landed gentleman and poetaster, was writing the biography of Cowper and required Blake's services as engraver and illustrator. In spite of the charms of country life Blake found the arrangement both irksome and humiliating, and the episode ended disastrously when he forcibly ejected an unknown dragoon from his garden and the latter then retaliated by accusing Blake of hair-raising seditious utterances. The charge was taken to court and it was many months before Blake was able to establish his innocence. By then (1804) the Blakes had returned to London and a period of neglect and disappointment followed. An elaborate exhibition of his pictures that Blake organized in the family shop in 1809 was a complete fiasco, and there was little or no public interest in the last and most ambitious of the Prophetic Books—*Milton* (1804–8) and *Jerusalem* (1804–20). His final years were sweetened, however, by the affection and admiration of a group of younger artists, which included Samuel Palmer, George Richmond and John Linnell. (It was Linnell's generosity, really, that kept Blake alive.) He died in London on August 12th, 1827, singing (as Tatham records) 'Hallelujahs and songs of joy and triumph which Mrs. Blake described as being truly sublime in music and in verse', until the walls rang and resounded.

III

Blake's mental or spiritual biography is less easy to summarize. Although it has recently been demonstrated that he was in closer touch with the day-to-day political and social realities of his time than anybody had suspected,[1] the child's fantasy-world of intensely vivid angels and prophets, with giant serpents and demonic horrors lurking in its shadows, remained with him to the end of his life. It is true the child's confusion of subjective 'visions' with phenomenal actualities was soon outgrown. All that Blake claimed for himself as 'visionary' was that the training he had given his imagination enabled him to *project* what his inner eye saw into the external world. But in the course of the projection he retained a full consciousness all the time, as he insisted, that Sir William Wallace, or the flea's ghost, or whatever the image was, was not 'really' there. 'You have the same faculty as I,' he used to tell his artist friends (according to Gilchrist), 'only you do not trust or cultivate it. You can see what I do, *if you choose*. . . .'

The legend among his contemporaries of Blake's madness—which was accepted even by Wordsworth, though he immediately added, 'there is something in the madness of this man which interests me more than the sanity of Lord Byron and Walter Scott'—was primarily due to Blake's habit of dramatizing

[1] See David V. Erdman, *Blake: Prophet against Empire*, Princeton, 1954. The notes in this edition are heavily indebted to Mr. Erdman's monumental scholarship.

his visions. A typical example of this innocent perversity is recorded by Allan Cunningham:

> Another friend, on whose veracity I have the fullest dependence, called one evening on Blake, and found him sitting with a pencil and a panel, drawing a portrait with all the seeming anxiety of a man who is conscious that he has got a fastidious sitter; he looked and drew and looked, yet no living soul was visible. 'Disturb me not,' said he, in a whisper, 'I have one sitting to me.' 'Sitting to you!' exclaimed his astonished visitor, where is he, and what is he? —I see no one.' 'But I see him, sir,' answered Blake haughtily, 'there he is, his name is Lot—you may read of him in the Scripture. *He* is sitting for his portrait.'

There is something pathetic in such anecdotes, which seem to accumulate towards the end of his life. The refusal of the world of culture and art to accept his visions for what they really were —symbolic expressions of a profoundly original philosophy of life—had made him *force* them on their attention by these little comedies. In his more responsible moods, Blake cannot have taken them seriously—nor need we.

A more serious temptation to which Blake, like other visionaries, was always exposed was to let the inner and outer worlds co-exist as parallel realities without ever coming into any actual contact with each other. The later poems often reflect some such a semi-neurotic condition. There is, for instance, a revealing scrap of versified autobiography that Blake sent Flaxman just before going to Felpham in 1800 ('I know you will be pleased with the intention, and hope you will forgive the poetry'):

> I bless thee, O Father of Heaven and Earth! that ever I saw Flaxman's face:
> Angels stand round my spirit in Heaven; the blessed of Heaven are my friends upon Earth.
> When Flaxman was taken to Italy [1787], Fuseli was given to me for a season;

And now Flaxman hath given me Hayley, his friend, to be mine—
such my lot upon Earth!
Now my lot in the Heavens is this: Milton loved me in childhood
and showed me his face:
Ezra came with Isaiah the Prophet, but Shakespeare in riper years
gave me his hand;
Paracelsus and Boehmen appeared to me; terrors appeared in the
Heavens above;
The American War began; all its dark horrors passed before my
face
Across the Atlantic to France; then the French Revolution com-
menced in thick clouds;
And my Angels have told me that, seeing such visions, I could not
subsist on the Earth,
But by my conjunction with Flaxman, who knows to forgive
nervous fear.

It is impossible not to be touched by the simple sincerity of
these lines, but their hard and fast division between the friends
on Earth (Flaxman, Fuseli, Hayley) and the friends in Heaven
(Milton, Ezra, Isaiah, Shakespeare, Paracelsus, Boehme) is
typical of the uncritical simplifications that vitiate the Prophetic
Books. In sober human fact the terrestrial and celestial friendships
had been closely connected, but Blake has ignored or suppressed
the names of the two essential links—Emanuel Swedenborg,
the Swedish mystic-cum-mineralogist, and Johann Kaspar
Lavater, the Swiss moralist-cum-physiognomist. It had been
Flaxman who introduced Blake to Swedenborgianism, and the
reading of one of Swedenborg's treatises and Fuseli's excellent
translation of Lavater—on both of which Blake entered a large
number of extremely acute marginal comments—may be said
to mark his intellectual coming of age. That was in 1788-9.
And by this time Blake was one of a group of social and political
radicals—Thomas Holcroft, Mary Wollstonecraft, Tom Paine,
and others, as well as Fuseli himself—who attended the weekly
dinners provided by the genial Joseph Johnson, of St. Paul's

Churchyard, their printer, publisher and friend. In these stimulating surroundings Blake was able to work out his own drastic conclusions about orthodox Christianity, Swedenborgianism (which he soon outgrew), and the American and French Revolutions. Milton, Ezra and Isaiah 'in the Heavens' were important to him because they provided the imagery and symbols that enabled him to think out those conclusions (it is this *necessity* to think in images that distinguishes Blake from a man like William Godwin); Paracelsus and Boehme partly for the same reason, as sources of imagery, but principally because they provided examples of the actual mechanism of symbolic thinking.

The most important of the symbolic mechanisms, one that Blake derives largely from Boehme, is what may be called the Doctrine of Contraries. The Doctrine is defined in an early passage of *The Marriage of Heaven and Hell* (1790–3): 'Without Contraries is no progression. Attraction and repulsion, reason and energy, love and hate, are necessary to human existence.' A longer passage in the same work elaborates this concept of necessary oppositions in terms of a 'Prolific' force and a 'Devouring' force:

> To the Devourer it seems as if the Producer was in his chains; but it is not so, he only takes portions of existence and fancies that the whole.
>
> But the Prolific would cease to be prolific unless the Devourer, as a sea, received the excess of his delights. Some will say: 'Is not God alone the Prolific?' I answer: 'God only acts and is in existing beings, or men.'
>
> These two classes of men are always upon earth, and they should be enemies: whoever tries to reconcile them seeks to destroy existence.
>
> Religion is an endeavour to reconcile the two.

It is clear that the only 'progression' there can be in such a universe is cyclical—a period of excessive prolificness followed by a period in which the Devourer has it all his own way. And, in fact, Blake's later mythology is dominated by cycles of disintegration and re-integration. In *The Marriage of Heaven and Hell* the emphasis is not on cycles but on oppositions, and it is ethical rather than metaphysical or psychological. The crime of 'religion', the conventional Protestantism of the eighteenth century, was its attempt 'to destroy existence' by ignoring or minimizing the essential oppositions in human nature, a process that entailed reducing the rational faculty to arithmetic and the emotions to sentimentality. The morality that based itself on such reductions—the morality of 'Thou shalt not'—seemed to Blake nothing less than conscious or unconscious hypocrisy. Hence such 'Proverbs of Hell' as 'Prudence is a rich ugly old maid courted by incapacity', or 'Sooner murder an infant in its cradle than nurse unacted desires'.

But the Contraries of *The Marriage of Heaven and Hell* are a little naïve. The essential Blake is not there but in *Songs of Innocence and of Experience* and the associated lyrics. The relationship between the two series of songs is defined on their general title-page (reproduced as the frontispiece to this edition): 'the two Contrary States of the Human Soul'. In the case of the Songs of Innocence the demonstration was necessarily an *ex post facto* one, since they had been written and engraved before the Doctrine of Contraries had been worked out. But, though not explicitly contemplated as the opposite of Experience, Innocence is, of course, a recognizable state of the human soul. Its popular name is Happiness. By confronting Innocence, song by song, with an opposite that every reader will recognize as true by his own Experience, Blake has in fact conducted a most searching investigation into the limitations and conditions of human satisfactions.

The emotional tensions between the two Contrary States have a revealing biographical background. The Songs of Innocence were the product of the early years of Blake's marriage, and they reflect his happy excitement in having found someone who could share his fantasy-world with him and help him to relate it to human realities. The gay realism of *An Island in the Moon*, which was written some fifteen months only after the marriage, is a measure of Kate's success. Some of the Songs of Innocence were also written at this time, perhaps in part at any rate for the children he and Kate hoped they would soon have (it was, in fact, a childless marriage). The Songs of Experience, on the other hand, were the outcome of a later period of dissension and marital jealousy. Exactly what went wrong in the marriage is not known, but *My Pretty Rose-tree*, which is the first poem in a precious notebook that contains, along with sketches and miscellaneous jottings, early drafts of most of the Songs of Experience, appears to tell in symbolic form a story of amorous advances made to Blake by some 'Such a flower as May never bore' (who may or may not have been Mary Wollstonecraft[1]), their rejection by him, and his puzzled distress

[1] Mary Wollstonecraft did undoubtedly make precisely such advances to Fuseli early in 1792, though the Victorian members of the Shelley family have done their best to hush up their grandmother's indiscretion. (See R. M. Wardle, *Mary Wollstonecraft: a Critical Biography*, 1951, p. 350.) But the sudden interest in her clothes and appearance, which surprised and amused her friends and relations before it led to the infatuation with Fuseli, had begun in 1791. And all the qualities of mind and heart that made the ugly middle-aged Fuseli so irresistible were present in far greater measure in Blake, who was also her own age. Granted that Mary would be seeing both of them constantly at Johnson's dinners and elsewhere, the balance of psychological probability is that an abortive flirtation with Blake may have preceded the affair with Fuseli. At this time, in the full bloom of her not inconsiderable beauty and with *A Vindication of the Rights of Woman* in actual process of composition (it was published early in 1792), she was indeed 'Such a flower as May never bore'. In any case Mary Wollstonecraft's unorthodox opinions are often strikingly similar to Blake's. Thus her dictum 'children are taught revenge and lies in their very cradles' (*Thoughts on the Education of Daughters*, 1787, p. 9) anticipates *A Cradle Song* (Experience). Two 'Hints' intended for a second part of *The Rights of Woman* are 'while women are encouraged to ornament their persons at the expense of their minds, while indolence renders them helpless and lascivious (for what other name can be given to the common intercourse between the sexes?) they will be, generally speaking, only objects of desire' (*Posthumous Works*, 1798, iv. 183), and 'A writer of genius makes us feel; an inferior author reason' (*ibid.*, p. 195).

when he discovered that Kate, instead of congratulating him upon his constancy,

> turned away with jealousy,
> And her thorns were my only delight.

No doubt the poem has simplified what actually occurred. Advances are not made unless there has been some encouraging look or hint from the other party. And in any case Kate's jealousy —she was already thirty in 1791, the probable date of the episode, and no intellectual at the best of times—would be natural and forgivable. But to Blake, for whom the essence of love was the freedom it created from all other obligations, her behaviour came as a shattering shock. Kate's jealousy, as he interpreted it, only went to show that she too shared the commercial morality of the chartered streets. By their marriage contract his sexual liberty, one of the most precious and private things in life, had become *her* property, *her* legal possession!

The sin of jealousy, with the associated moral problem of the power that sexual love can give a woman over a man, is a recurring topic in Blake's later poems. But by that time his distress had become generalized and depersonalized. In the poems in the notebook immediately following *My Pretty Rose-tree* he can be seen adjusting himself to his crisis, at first reacting angrily against it, and then slowly working out its implications. This is the mood of 'Never seek to tell thy love', *The Clod and the Pebble*, 'I laid me down upon a bank', *The Garden of Love*, 'I saw a chapel all of gold', and 'I asked a thief to steal me a peach'—the six powerful but intensely bitter poems that come next in the notebook. Even in these poems, however, the bitterness is not directed against Kate so much as against woman-kind in general and the hypocritical moral code that will not permit women to behave naturally and generously. It is only with the eighth poem in the notebook, an early version of *The*

Human Image, that there comes the first suggestion of a Contrary State:

> Mercy could be no more
> If there was nobody poor,
> And Pity no more could be
> If all were as happy as we.

The reference here to *The Divine Image* in *Songs of Innocence*, a poem that had celebrated the Christian virtues of Mercy, Pity, Peace and Love, is clear and explicit. So this, Blake is saying to himself, is Mercy and Pity in the light of Experience! And from that realization it was only a step to the recognition of a *general* condition logically and emotionally antithetical to Innocence. From this point, with the Doctrine of Contraries now providing a theoretical framework within which his personal agony and rebellion can generalize themselves, the poetry of Experience loses most of its personal bitterness. *A Poison Tree* is on the same page of the notebook, and within another page or two he is writing *London*, *The Tiger* and *The Sick Rose*.

IV

Blake was thirty-three or at the most thirty-four when he wrote these poems. With the exception of '*Ah! Sunflower*' and 'Hear the voice of the Bard', which were apparently written rather later than the other Songs of Experience, and the familiar and much later lyric in *Milton*, 'And did those feet in ancient time', he was to write no more poetry that is indisputably first class. His case is different, however, from Wordsworth's and Coleridge's, who had also written all their greatest poetry by the same age, in one significant respect. It is that Blake made no attempt for a number of years to write any lyric poetry at all. Instead, all his literary energies were diverted into the composition of his Prophetic Books. As no extracts have been included in this edition from these works—apart from the epilogue from

The Marriage of Heaven and Hell and three lyrics from *Milton* and *Jerusalem*—it will not be necessary to do more than glance at the special and extremely intricate problems that they raise. Modern research has demonstrated that the Prophetic Books are more coherent and intelligible than Blake's early critics thought, and the reader who is prepared to learn Blake's peculiar idiom—which is not so much a matter of memorizing the names and relationships of his principal mythological figures as of adjusting himself to an allegory that operates on several symbolic levels at the same time—will be amply rewarded. But an exceptional ability is demanded to suspend conventional disbeliefs. By normal standards the Prophetic Books are very badly written. One's first impression, especially with the later books, is of poems written much too fast and insufficiently revised. The tighter form of the lyric—with its short lines, its regular recurrence of rhyme and its simple dramatic structure—provided an incomparably superior literary framework for Blake's poetry, even when it is at its most didactic. The Voice of the Bard is generally much too loud, too verbose and too diffuse. As long as he was writing lyrics, the folk-song tradition—which Blake elaborated and extended but never completely deserted —imposed its own models of tact and restraint. The symbols— the rose, the lily, the pebble of the brook, the lion, the fly, the garden, the apple, etc.—remain earthbound. Consider, for example, the following medieval folk-song, which is surely an embryonic Song of Experience:

> All night by the rose, rose,
>   All night by the rose I lay;
> Darf [=need] I naught the rose to steal,
>   And yet I bore the flower away.

The implied reference to such popular symbols keeps Blake's lyrics within the main current of English poetry. The Prophetic Books, on the other hand, with their sources and points of reference in Jewish mysticism, Renaissance alchemy, Early Christian heresies, Hindu religion, and eighteenth-century fantasies about the Druids, are exotic phenomena. Their relative success, therefore, is all the more remarkable. With every reason why they should fail, in their turgidity, their obscurity and their pretentiousness, they unquestionably succeed—provided, that is, they are taken on their own peculiar terms. They have even one advantage over the lyrics in the superior force, beauty and relevance of the engraved illustrations and decorations. Blake was slower to find himself as pictorial artist than as poet, and the illustrations to *Songs of Innocence*—and indeed to most of the *Songs of Experience* too—add little to the essential meaning of the poems. In one or two instances they are actually misleading, whereas in *The Marriage of Heaven and Hell*, *America*, *Europe*, *The Book of Urizen* and *Jerusalem*, and the other prophecies, too, to a lesser degree, the illustrations are a superb complement to the texts.

But the proper way to approach Blake's Prophetic Books is *through* the lyrics. In this selection the reader will find a miniature foretaste of what awaits him there in 'A Song of Liberty' from *The Marriage of Heaven and Hell*, which is an excellent specimen of Blake's prophetic manner. Its poetic prose is perhaps preferable to the loose accentual verse—with anything from four to eight stresses in the line—in which all the others are written. And many of the complexities of prophetic symbolism are illustrated in such later lyrics as *The Golden Net* and *The Mental Traveller*. A gap, however, of some years divides the last of the Songs of Experience from these lyrics. Since Blake's intellectual evolution in this interval can only be defined in terms of the Prophetic Books, that are all that survive from it—apart from the magnificent colour prints of 1795, some paintings and sketches, and a few letters—there will be no need to attempt it here. It can perhaps be summarized as a gradual transition from social and political prophecy (*Visions of the Daughters of Albion* and *America*, both engraved in 1793) to a mystical psychology (*The Four Zoas*, first version 1797), the change reflecting Blake's disillusionment as to the potentialities of revolution and culminating in a total distrust of the world of the senses. In or about 1800 Blake returned, on his own unorthodox terms, to the Christianity against which he had revolted ten years before, and his last poem is a restatement, in characteristically paradoxical form, of the Sermon on the Mount.

A few of the later epigrams have also been included in this selection. They provide an amusing Contrary to the solemn didactics of the Prophetic Books and sometimes illustrate the refreshingly human irritability of which Blake's closest friends (such as Flaxman) occasionally complained.

POEMS

SELECTED LYRICS
FROM 'POETICAL SKETCHES'

To the Muses

Whether on Ida's shady brow,
Or in the chambers of the East,
The chambers of the sun, that now
From ancient melody have ceased;

Whether in Heaven ye wander fair,   5
Or the green corners of the earth,
Or the blue regions of the air
Where the melodious winds have birth;

Whether on crystal rocks ye rove,
Beneath the bosom of the sea   10
Wandering in many a coral grove,
Fair Nine, forsaking Poetry!

How have you left the ancient love
That bards of old enjoyed in you!
The languid strings do scarcely move!   15
The sound is forced, the notes are few!

Song

My silks and fine array,
My smiles and languished air,
By love are driven away;
And mournful lean Despair
Brings me yew to deck my grave;
Such end true lovers have.

His face is fair as heaven
When springing buds unfold;
O! why to him was't given
Whose heart is wintry cold? 10
His breast is love's all-worshipped tomb.
Where all love's pilgrims come.

Bring me an axe and spade,
Bring me a winding-sheet;
When I my grave have made 15
Let winds and tempests beat:
Then down I'll lie as cold as clay.
True love doth pass away!

Song

Memory, hither come,
And tune your merry notes:
And, while upon the wind
Your music floats,
I'll pore upon the stream 5
Where sighing lovers dream,
And fish for fancies as they pass
Within the watery glass.

I'll drink of the clear stream,
And hear the linnet's song; 10
And there I'll lie and dream
The day along:
And when night comes, I'll go
To places fit for woe,
Walking along the darkened valley 15
With silent Melancholy.

2

To Spring

O thou with dewy locks, who lookest down
Thro' the clear windows of the morning, turn
Thine angel eyes upon our western isle,
Which in full choir hails thy approach, O Spring!

The hills tell each other, and the listening   5
Valleys hear; all our longing eyes are turned
Up to thy bright pavilions: issue forth,
And let thy holy feet visit our clime.

Come o'er the eastern hills, and let our winds
Kiss thy perfumed garments; let us taste   10
Thy morn and evening breath; scatter thy pearls
Upon our love-sick land that mourns for thee.

O deck her forth with thy fair fingers; pour
Thy soft kisses on her bosom; and put
Thy golden crown upon her languished head,   15
Whose modest tresses were bound up for thee.

To Summer

O thou who passest thro' our valleys in
Thy strength, curb thy fierce steeds, allay the heat
That flames from their large nostrils! Thou, O Summer,
Oft pitched'st here thy golden tent, and oft
Beneath our oaks hast slept, while we beheld   5
With joy thy ruddy limbs and flourishing hair.

3

Beneath our thickest shades we oft have heard
Thy voice, when noon upon his fervid car
Rode o'er the deep of heaven; beside our springs
Sit down, and in our mossy valleys, on   10
Some bank beside a river clear, throw thy
Silk draperies off, and rush into the stream:
Our valleys love the Summer in his pride.

Our bards are famed who strike the silver wire:
Our youth are bolder than the southern swains: 15
Our maidens fairer in the sprightly dance:
We lack not songs, nor instruments of joy,
Nor echoes sweet, nor waters clear as heaven,
Nor laurel wreaths against the sultry heat.

To Autumn

O Autumn! laden with fruit, and stained
With the blood of the grape, pass not, but sit
Beneath my shady roof; there thou may'st rest,
And tune thy jolly voice to my fresh pipe,
And all the daughters of the year shall dance!   5
Sing now the lusty song of fruits and flowers.

'The narrow bud opens her beauties to
The sun, and love runs in her thrilling veins;
Blossoms hang round the brows of morning, and
Flourish down the bright cheek of modest eve,   10
Till clustering summer breaks forth into singing,
And feathered clouds strew flowers round her head.

4

'The spirits of the air live on the smells
Of fruit; and joy, with pinions light, roves round
The gardens, or sits singing in the trees.'   15
Thus sang the jolly Autumn as he sat;
Then rose, girded himself, and o'er the bleak
Hills fled from our sight; but left his golden load.

To Winter

'O Winter! bar thine adamantine doors:
The north is thine; there hast thou built thy dark
Deep-founded habitation. Shake not thy roofs,
Nor bend thy pillars with thine iron car.'

He hears me not, but o'er the yawning deep   5
Rides heavy; his storms are unchained, sheathed
In ribbed steel; I dare not lift mine eyes,
For he hath reared his sceptre o'er the world.

Lo! now the direful monster, whose skin clings
To his strong bones, strides o'er the groaning rocks: 10
He withers all in silence, and his hand
Unclothes the earth, and freezes up frail life.

He takes his seat upon the cliffs,—the mariner
Cries in vain. Poor little wretch, that deal'st
With storms!—till heaven smiles, and the monster   15
Is driven yelling to his caves beneath mount Hecla.

Mad Song

The wild winds weep,
And the night is a-cold;
Come hither, Sleep,
And my griefs enfold:
But lo! the morning peeps   5
Over the eastern steeps,
And the rustling birds of dawn
The earth do scorn.

Lo! to the vault
Of pavèd heaven,   10
With sorrow fraught
My notes are driven:
They strike the ear of night,
Make weep the eyes of day;
They make mad the roaring winds,   15
And with tempests play.

Like a fiend in a cloud,
With howling woe
After night I do crowd,
And with night will go;   20
I turn my back to the east
From whence comforts have increased;
For light doth seize my brain
With frantic pain.

Song

How sweet I roamed from field to field
And tasted all the summer's pride,
Till I the Prince of Love beheld
Who in the sunny beams did glide!

He showed me lilies for my hair,   5
And blushing roses for my brow;
He led me through his gardens fair
Where all his golden pleasures grow.

With sweet May dews my wings were wet,
And Phoebus fired my vocal rage;   10
He caught me in his silken net,
And shut me in his golden cage.

He loves to sit and hear me sing,
Then, laughing, sports and plays with me;
Then stretches out my golden wing,   15
And mocks my loss of liberty.

Song

Love and harmony combine,
And around our souls entwine
While thy branches mix with mine,
And our roots together join.

Joys upon our branches sit, 5
Chirping loud and singing sweet;
Like gentle streams beneath our feet
Innocence and virtue meet.

Thou the golden fruit dost bear,
I am clad in flowers fair; 10
Thy sweet boughs perfume the air,
And the turtle buildeth there.

There she sits and feeds her young,
Sweet I hear her mournful song;
And thy lovely leaves among, 15
There is Love, I hear his tongue.

There his charming nest doth lay,
There he sleeps the night away;
There he sports along the day,
And doth among our branches play. 20

EXTRACTS FROM

AN ISLAND IN THE MOON

In the Moon is a certain Island near by a mighty continent, which small island seems to have some affinity to England, & what is more extraordinary, the people are so much alike, & their language so much the same, that you would think you was among your friends. In this Island dwells three Philosophers— Suction the Epicurean, Quid the Cynic, & Sipsop the Pythagorean. I call them by the names of those sects, tho' the sects are not ever mention'd there, as being quite out of date; however, the things still remain, and the vanities are the same. The three Philosophers sat together thinking of nothing. In comes Etruscan Column the Antiquarian, & after an abundance of Enquiries to no purpose, sat himself down & described something that nobody listen'd to. So they were employ'd when Mrs. Gimblet came in. The corners of her mouth seem'd—I don't know how, but very odd, as if she hoped you had not an ill opinion of her,— to be sure, we are all poor creatures! Well, she seated [herself] & seem'd to listen with great attention while the Antiquarian, seem'd to be talking of virtuous cats. But it was not so; she was thinking of the shape of her eyes & mouth, & he was thinking of his eternal fame. The three Philosophers at this time were each endeavouring to conceal his laughter (not at them but) at his own imagination.

This was the situation of this improving company when, in a great hurry, Inflammable Gass the Wind-finder enter'd. They seem'd to rise & salute each other. Etruscan Column & Inflammable Gass fix'd their eyes on each other; their tongues went in question & answer, but their thoughts were otherwise employ'd. 'I don't like his eyes,' said Etruscan Column. 'He's a foolish puppy,' said Inflammable Gass, smiling on him. The 3 Philoso-phers—the Cynic smiling, the Epicurean seeming studying the flame of the candle, & the Pythagorean playing with the cat—listen'd with open mouths to the edifying discourses.

'Sir,' said the Antiquarian, 'I have seen these works, & I do affirm that they are no such thing. They seem to me to be the most wretched, paltry, flimsy stuff that ever——'

'What d'ye say? What d'ye say?' said Inflammable Gass. 'Why—why, I wish I could see you write so.'

'Sir,' said the Antiquarian, 'according to my opinion the author is an errant blockhead.'

'Your reason—Your reason?' said Inflammable Gass. 'Why—why, I think it very abominable to call a man a blockhead that you know nothing of.'

'Reason, Sir?' said the Antiquarian. 'I'll give you an example for your reason. As I was walking along the street I saw a vast number of swallows on the rails of an old Gothic square. They seem'd to be going on their passage, as Pliny says. As I was looking up, a little *outré* fellow, pulling me by the sleeve, cries, "Pray, Sir, who do all they belong to?" I turn'd myself about with great contempt. Said I, "Go along, you fool!" "Fool!" said he, "who do you call fool? I only ask'd you a civil question." I had a great mind to have thrash'd the fellow, only he was bigger than I.'

Here Etruscan Column left off—Inflammable Gass, recollecting himself [said], 'Indeed I do not think the man was a fool, for he seems to me to have been desirous of enquiring into the works of nature!'

'Ha! Ha! Ha!' said the Pythagorean.

It was re-echo'd by Inflammable Gass to overthrow the argument.

Etruscan Column then, starting up & clenching both his fists, was prepared to give a formal answer to the company. But Obtuse Angle, entering the room, having made a gentle bow, proceeded to empty his pockets of a vast number of papers, turned about & sat down, wiped his face with his pocket handkerchief, & shutting his eyes, began to scratch his head.

'Well, gentlemen,' said he, 'what is the cause of strife?'

The Cynic answer'd, 'They are only quarreling about Voltaire.'

'Yes' said the Epicurean, '& having a bit of fun with him.'

'And,' said the Pythagorean, 'endeavoring to incorporate their souls with their bodies.'

Obtuse Angle, giving a grin, said, 'Voltaire understood nothing of the Mathematics, and a man must be a fool i'faith not to understand the Mathematics.'

Inflammable Gass, turning round hastily in his chair, said, 'Mathematics! He found out a number of Queries in Philosophy.'

Obtuse Angle, shutting his eyes & saying that he always understood better when he shut his eyes, [replied], 'In the first place, it is no use for a man to make Queries, but to solve them; for a man may be a fool & make Queries, but a man must have good sound sense to solve them. A query & an answer are as different as a strait line & a crooked one. Secondly——'

'I—I—I—aye! Secondly, Voltaire's a fool,' says the Epicurean.

'Pooh!' says the Mathematician, scratching his head with double violence, 'It is not worth Quarreling about.'

The Antiquarian here got up, &, hemming twice to shew the strength of his Lungs, said, 'But, my Good Sir, Voltaire was immersed in matter, & seems to have understood very little but what he saw before his eyes, like the Animal upon the Pythagorean's lap, always playing with its own tail.'

'Ha! Ha! Ha!' said Inflammable Gass. 'He was the Glory of France. I have got a bottle of air that would spread a Plague.'

Here the Antiquarian shrugg'd up his shoulders, & was silent while Inflammable Gass talk'd for half an hour.

When Steelyard, the lawgiver, coming in stalking—with an

act of parliament in his hand, said that it was a shameful thing that acts of parliament should be in a free state, it had so engrossed his mind that he did not salute the company.

Mrs. Gimblet drew her mouth downwards.

CHAP 2d

Tilly Lally, the Siptippidist, Aradobo, the Dean of Morocco, Miss Gittipin, Mrs. Nannicantipot, Mrs. Sistagatist, Gibble Gabble, the wife of Inflammable Gass, & Little Scopprell enter'd the room.

(If I have not presented you with every character in the piece, call me Ass.)

*   *   *   *   *   *   *

CHAP 6

They all went home & left the Philosophers. Then Suction Ask'd if Pindar was not a better Poet than Ghiotto was a Painter.

'Plutarch has not the life of Ghiotto,' said Sipsop.

'No,' said Quid, 'to be sure, he was an Italian.'

'Well,' said Suction, 'that is not any proof.'

'Plutarch was a nasty ignorant puppy,' said Quid. 'I hate your sneaking rascals. There's Aradobo in ten or twelve years will be a far superior genius.'

'Ah!' said the Pythagorean, 'Aradobo will make a very clever fellow.'

'Why,' said Quid, 'I think that any natural fool would make a clever fellow, if he was properly brought up.'

'Ah, hang your reasoning!' said the Epicurean. 'I hate reasoning. I do everything by my feelings.'

'Ah!' said Sipsop, 'I only wish Jack Tearguts had had the

cutting of Plutarch. He understands Anatomy better than any of the Ancients. He'll plunge his knife up to the hilt in a single drive and thrust his fist in, and all in the space of a Quarter of an hour. He does not mind their crying, tho' they cry ever so. He'll swear at them & keep them down with his fist, & tell them that he'll scrape their bones if they don't lay still & be quiet. What the devil should the people in the hospital that have it done for nothing make such a piece of work for?'

'Hang that,' said Suction; 'let us have a song.'

Then the Cynic sang—

1.

'When old corruption first begun,
   Adorn'd in yellow vest,
He committed on flesh a whoredom—
   O, what a wicked beast!

2.

From them a callow babe did spring,
   And old corruption smil'd
To think his race should never end,
   For now he had a child.

3.

He call'd him surgery, & fed
   The babe with his own milk,
For flesh & he could ne'er agree,
   She would not let him suck.

4.

And this he always kept in mind,
   And form'd a crooked knife,
And ran about with bloody hands
   To seek his mother's life.

5.

And as he ran to seek his mother
   He met with a dead woman,
He fell in love & married her,
   A deed which is not common.

6.

She soon grew pregnant & brought forth
   Scurvy & spott'd fever.
The father grin'd & skipt about,
   And said, "I'm made for ever!"

7.

"For now I have procur'd these imps
   I'll try experiments."
With that he tied poor scurvy down
   & stopt up all its vents.

8.

And when the child began to swell,
   He shouted out aloud,
"I've found the dropsy out, & soon,
   Shall do the world more good."

9.

He took up fever by the neck
   And cut out all its spots,
And thro' the holes which he had made
   He first discover'd guts.'

'Ah,' said Sipsop, 'you think we are rascals—& we think you are rascals. I do as I chuse. What is it to any body what I do? I am always unhappy too. When I think of Surgery—I don't know. I do it because I like it. My father does what he likes & so do I. I think, somehow, I'll leave it off. There was a woman having her cancer cut, & she shriekd'd so that I was quite sick.'

SONGS OF
INNOCENCE AND OF EXPERIENCE

Introduction

(*Songs of Innocence*)

Piping down the valleys wild,
Piping songs of pleasant glee,
On a cloud I saw a child,
And he laughing said to me:

'Pipe a song about a Lamb!'   5
So I piped with merry cheer.
'Piper, pipe that song again.'
So I piped: he wept to hear.

'Drop thy pipe, thy happy pipe;
Sing thy songs of happy cheer.'   10
So I sung the same again,
While he wept with joy to hear.

'Piper, sit thee down and write
In a book, that all may read.'
So he vanished from my sight,   15
And I plucked a hollow reed,

And I made a rural pen,
And I stained the water clear,
And I wrote my happy songs
Every child may joy to hear.   20

Introduction

(*Songs of Experience*)

Hear the voice of the Bard!
Who present, past, and future sees;
Whose ears have heard
The Holy Word,
That walked among the ancient trees,   5

Calling the lapsèd soul,
And weeping in the evening dew;
That might control
The starry pole,
And fallen, fallen light renew!   10

'O Earth, O Earth, return!
Arise from out the dewy grass;
Night is worn,
And the morn
Rises from the slumberous mass.   15

'Turn away no more;
Why wilt thou turn away?
The starry floor,
The watery shore,
Is given thee till the break of day.'   20

Earth's Answer

(*Experience*)

Earth raised up her head
From the darkness dread and drear,
Her light fled
(Stony dread!),
And her locks covered with grey despair.   5

'Prisoned on watery shore,
Starry Jealousy does keep my den:
Cold and hoar,
Weeping o'er,
I hear the Father of the Ancient Men.   10

'Selfish Father of Men!
Cruel, jealous, selfish Fear!
Can delight,
Chained in night,
The virgins of youth and morning bear?   15

'Does spring hide its joy
When buds and blossoms grow?
Does the sower
Sow by night,
Or the ploughman in darkness plough?   20

'Break this heavy chain
That does freeze my bones around.
Selfish! vain!
Eternal bane!
That free Love with bondage bound.'   25

A Cradle Song

(*Innocence*)

Sweet dreams, form a shade
O'er my lovely infant's head;
Sweet dreams of pleasant streams
By happy, silent, moony beams.

Sweet sleep, with soft down   5
Weave thy brows an infant crown.
Sweet sleep, Angel mild,
Hover o'er my happy child.

Sweet smiles, in the night,
Hover over my delight;   10
Sweet smiles, mother's smiles,
All the livelong night beguiles.

Sweet moans, dovelike sighs,
Chase not slumber from thy eyes.
Sweet moans, sweeter smiles,   15
All the dovelike moans beguiles.

Sleep, sleep, happy child,
All creation slept and smiled;
Sleep, sleep, happy sleep,
While o'er thee thy mother weep.   20

Sweet babe, in thy face
Holy image I can trace.
Sweet babe, once like thee,
Thy Maker lay and wept for me,

Wept for me, for thee, for all,   25
When He was an infant small.

Thou His image ever see,
Heavenly face that smiles on thee,

Smiles on thee, on me, on all;
Who became an infant small.　　　　　30
Infant smiles are His own smiles;
Heaven and earth to peace beguiles.

A Cradle Song

(*Experience*)

Sleep! sleep! beauty bright,
Dreaming o'er the joys of night;
Sleep! sleep! in thy sleep
Little sorrows sit and weep.

Sweet Babe, in thy face　　　　　　　5
Soft desires I can trace,
Secret joys and secret smiles,
Little pretty infant wiles.

As thy softest limbs I feel,
Smiles as of the morning steal　　　　10
O'er thy cheek, and o'er thy breast
Where thy little heart does rest.

O! the cunning wiles that creep
In thy little heart asleep.
When thy little heart does wake　　　15
Then the dreadful lightnings break,

From thy cheek and from thy eye,
O'er the youthful harvests nigh.
Infant wiles and infant smiles
Heaven and Earth of peace beguiles.　20

Infant Joy

(*Innocence*)

'I have no name:
I am but two days old.'
What shall I call thee?
'I happy am,
Joy is my name.'   5
Sweet joy befall thee!

Pretty Joy!
Sweet Joy, but two days old!
Sweet Joy I call thee.
Thou dost smile,   10
I sing the while,
Sweet joy befall thee!

Infant Sorrow

(*Experience*)

My mother groaned, my father wept,
Into the dangerous world I leapt;
Helpless, naked, piping loud,
Like a fiend hid in a cloud.

Struggling in my father's hands,   5
Striving against my swaddling-bands,
Bound and weary, I thought best
To sulk upon my mother's breast.

Nurse's Song

When the voices of children are heard on the green,
And laughing is heard on the hill,
My heart is at rest within my breast,
And everything else is still.

'Then come home, my children, the sun is gone down,   5
And the dews of night arise;
Come, come, leave off play, and let us away
Till the morning appears in the skies.'

'No, no, let us play, for it is yet day,
And we cannot go to sleep;   10
Besides, in the sky the little birds fly,
And the hills are all covered with sheep.'

'Well, well, go and play till the light fades away,
And then go home to bed.'
The little ones leaped and shouted and laughed   15
And all the hills echoèd.

Nurse's Song

When the voices of children are heard on the green
And whisperings are in the dale,
The days of my youth rise fresh in my mind,
My face turns green and pale.

Then come home, my children, the sun is gone down,   5
And the dews of night arise;
Your spring and your day are wasted in play,
And your winter and night in disguise.

The Lamb

(*Innocence*)

   Little Lamb, who made thee?
   Dost thou know who made thee?
Gave thee life, and bid thee feed,
By the stream and o'er the mead?
Gave thee clothing of delight,   5
Softest clothing, woolly, bright?
Gave thee such a tender voice,
Making all the vales rejoice?
   Little Lamb, who made thee?
   Dost thou know who made thee?   10

   Little Lamb, I'll tell thee,
   Little Lamb, I'll tell thee:
He is called by thy name,
For He calls Himself a Lamb.
He is meek, and He is mild;   15
He became a little child.
I a child, and thou a lamb,
We are called by His name.
   Little Lamb, God bless thee!
   Little Lamb, God bless thee!   20

The Tiger
(*Experience*)

Tiger! Tiger! burning bright
In the forests of the night,
What immortal hand or eye
Could frame thy fearful symmetry?

In what distant deeps or skies   5
Burnt the fire of thine eyes?
On what wings dare he aspire?
What the hand dare seize the fire?

And what shoulder, and what art,
Could twist the sinews of thy heart?   10
And when thy heart began to beat,
What dread hand, and what dread feet?

What the hammer? what the chain?
In what furnace was thy brain?
What the anvil? what dread grasp   15
Dare its deadly terrors clasp?

When the stars threw down their spears,
And watered heaven with their tears,
Did he smile his work to see?
Did he who made the Lamb make thee?   20

Tiger! Tiger! burning bright
In the forests of the night,
What immortal hand or eye,
Dare frame thy fearful symmetry?

The Blossom

(Innocence)

Merry, merry Sparrow!
Under leaves so green,
A happy blossom
Sees you, swift as arrow,
Seek your cradle narrow   5
Near my bosom.

Pretty, pretty Robin!
Under leaves so green,
A happy blossom
Hears you sobbing, sobbing,   10
Pretty, pretty Robin,
Near my bosom.

The Sick Rose

(Experience)

O Rose! thou art sick!
The invisible worm,
That flies in the night,
In the howling storm,

Has found out thy bed   5
Of crimson joy;
And his dark secret love
Does thy life destroy.

The Chimney Sweeper

(*Innocence*)

When my mother died I was very young,
And my father sold me while yet my tongue
Could scarcely cry "'weep! 'weep! 'weep! 'weep!'
So your chimneys I sweep, and in soot I sleep.

There's little Tom Dacre, who cried when his head,   5
That curled like a lamb's back, was shaved: so I said
'Hush, Tom! never mind it, for when your head's bare
You know that the soot cannot spoil your white hair.'

And so he was quiet, and that very night,
As Tom was a-sleeping, he had such a sight!—   10
That thousands of sweepers, Dick, Joe, Ned, and Jack,
Were all of them locked up in coffins of black.

And by came an Angel who had a bright key,
And he opened the coffins and set them all free;
Then down a green plain leaping, laughing, they run,   15
And wash in a river, and shine in the sun.

Then naked and white, all their bags left behind,
They rise upon clouds and sport in the wind;
And the Angel told Tom, if he'd be a good boy,
He'd have God for his father, and never want joy.   20

And so Tom awoke; and we rose in the dark,
And got with our bags and our brushes to work.
Tho' the morning was cold, Tom was happy and warm;
So if all do their duty they need not fear harm.

The Chimney Sweeper

(*Experience*)

A little black thing among the snow,
Crying "weep! 'weep!' in notes of woe!
'Where are thy father and mother, say?'—
'They are both gone up to the Church to pray.

'Because I was happy upon the heath,   5
And smiled among the winter's snow,
They clothed me in the clothes of death,
And taught me to sing the notes of woe.

'And because I am happy and dance and sing,
They think they have done me no injury,   10
And are gone to praise God and His Priest and King,
Who make up a Heaven of our misery.'

The Little Boy Lost

(*Innocence*)

'Father! father! where are you going?
O do not walk so fast.
Speak, father, speak to your little boy,
Or else I shall be lost.'

The night was dark, no father was there;   5
The child was wet with dew;
The mire was deep, and the child did weep,
And away the vapour flew.

The Little Boy Found

(*Innocence*)

The little boy lost in the lonely fen,
Led by the wandering light,
Began to cry; but God, ever nigh,
Appeared like his father, in white.

He kissed the child, and by the hand led,   5
And to his mother brought,
Who in sorrow pale, thro' the lonely dale,
Her little boy weeping sought.

A Little Boy Lost

(*Experience*)

'Nought loves another as itself,
Nor venerates another so,
Nor is it possible to Thought
A greater than itself to know:

'And, Father, how can I love you   5
Or any of my brothers more?
I love you like the little bird
That picks up crumbs around the door.'

The Priest sat by and heard the child,
In trembling zeal he seized his hair: 10
He led him by his little coat,
And all admired the priestly care.

And standing on the altar high,
'Lo! what a fiend is here,' said he,
'One who sets reason up for judge   15
Of our most holy Mystery.'

The weeping child could not be heard,
The weeping parents wept in vain;
They stripped him to his little shirt,
And bound him in an iron chain;   20

And burned him in a holy place,
Where many had been burned before:
The weeping parents wept in vain.
Are such things done on Albion's shore?

Holy Thursday

(*Innocence*)

'Twas on a Holy Thursday, their innocent faces clean,
The children walking two and two, in red and blue and green,
Grey-headed beadles walked before, with wands as white as snow,
Till into the high dome of Paul's they like Thames's waters flow.

O what a multitude they seemed, these flowers of London town! 5
Seated in companies they sit with radiance all their own.
The hum of multitudes was there, but multitudes of lambs,
Thousands of little boys and girls raising their innocent hands.

Now like a mighty wind they raise to Heaven the voice of song,
Or like harmonious thunderings the seats of Heaven among.   10
Beneath them sit the aged men, wise guardians of the poor;
Then cherish pity, lest you drive an angel from your door.

Holy Thursday

(*Experience*)

Is this a holy thing to see
In a rich and fruitful land,
Babes reduced to misery,
Fed with cold and usurous hand?

Is that trembling cry a song?   5
Can it be a song of joy?
And so many children poor?
It is a land of poverty!

And their sun does never shine,
And their fields are bleak and bare,   10
And their ways are filled with thorns:
It is eternal winter there.

For where'er the sun does shine,
And where'er the rain does fall,
Babe can never hunger there,
Nor poverty the mind appal.   15

A Dream

(*Innocence*)

Once a dream did weave a shade
O'er my Angel-guarded bed,
That an emmet lost its way
Where on grass methought I lay.

Troubled, 'wildered, and forlorn,   5
Dark, benighted, travel-worn,
Over many a tangled spray,
All heart-broke I heard her say:

'O, my children! do they cry?
Do they hear their father sigh?   10
Now they look abroad to see:
Now return and weep for me.'

Pitying, I dropped a tear;
But I saw a glow-worm near,
Who replied: 'What wailing wight   15
Calls the watchman of the night?

'I am set to light the ground,
While the beetle goes his round:
Follow now the beetle's hum;
Little wanderer, hie thee home.'   20

30

The Angel

(*Experience*)

I dreamt a dream! what can it mean?
And that I was a maiden Queen,
Guarded by an Angel mild:
Witless woe was ne'er beguiled!

And I wept both night and day,   5
And he wiped my tears away,
And I wept both day and night,
And hid from him my heart's delight.

So he took his wings and fled;
Then the morn blushed rosy red;   10
I dried my tears, and armed my fears
With ten thousand shields and spears.

Soon my Angel came again:
I was armed, he came in vain;
For the time of youth was fled,   15
And grey hairs were on my head.

The Divine Image

(*Innocence*)

To Mercy, Pity, Peace, and Love
All pray in their distress;
And to these virtues of delight
Return their thankfulness.

For Mercy, Pity, Peace, and Love   5
Is God, our Father dear,
And Mercy, Pity, Peace, and Love
Is man, His child and care.

For Mercy has a human heart,
Pity a human face,   10
And Love, the human form divine,
And Peace, the human dress.

Then every man, of every clime,
That prays in his distress,
Prays to the human form divine,   15
Love, Mercy, Pity, Peace.

And all must love the human form,
In heathen, Turk, or Jew;
Where Mercy, Love, and Pity dwell
There God is dwelling too.   20

The Human Image

(*Experience*)

Pity would be no more
If we did not make somebody **poor**;
And Mercy no more could be
If all were as happy as we.

And mutual fear brings peace,   5
Till the selfish loves increase;
Then Cruelty knits a snare,
And spreads his baits with care.

He sits down with holy fears,
And waters the ground with tears;   10
Then Humility takes its root
Underneath his foot.

Soon spreads the dismal shade
Of Mystery over his head;
And the caterpillar and fly   15
Feed on the Mystery.

And it bears the fruit of Deceit,
Ruddy and sweet to eat;
And the raven his nest has made
In its thickest shade.   20

The Gods of the earth and sea
Sought thro' nature to find this tree;
But their search was all in vain:
There grows one in the human brain.

Laughing Song

When the green woods laugh with the voice of joy,
And the dimpling stream runs laughing by;
When the air does laugh with our merry wit,
And the green hill laughs with the noise of it;

When the meadows laugh with lively green,   5
And the grasshopper laughs in the merry scene,
When Mary and Susan and Emily
With their sweet round mouths sing 'Ha, Ha, He!'

When the painted birds laugh in the shade,   10
Where our table with cherries and nuts is spread,
Come live, and be merry, and join with me,
To sing the sweet chorus of 'Ha, Ha, He!'

The Shepherd

How sweet is the Shepherd's sweet lot!
From the morn to the evening he strays;
He shall follow his sheep all the day,
And his tongue shall be filled with praise.

For he hears the lamb's innocent call,   5
And he hears the ewe's tender reply;
He is watchful, while they are in peace,
For they know when their Shepherd is nigh.

34

Spring

Sound the flute!
Now it's mute.
Birds delight
Day and night:
Nightingale   5
In the dale,
Lark in sky,
Merrily,
Merrily, merrily, to welcome in the year.

Little boy,   10
Full of joy;
Little girl,
Sweet and small;
Cock does crow,
So do you;   15
Merry voice,
Infant noise,
Merrily, merrily, to welcome in the year.

Little lamb,
Here I am;   20
Come and lick
My white neck;
Let me pull
Your soft wool;
Let me kiss   25
Your soft face:
Merrily, merrily, we welcome in the year.

The Echoing Green

The sun does arise,
And make happy the skies;
The merry bells ring
To welcome the spring;
The skylark and thrush,   5
The birds of the bush,
Sing louder around
To the bells' cheerful sound,
While our sports shall be seen
On the Echoing Green.   10

Old John with white hair,
Does laugh away care,
Sitting under the oak,
Among the old folk.
They laugh at our play,   15
And soon they all say:
'Such, such were the joys
When we all, girls and boys,
In our youth time were seen
On the Echoing Green.'   20

Till the little ones, weary,
No more can be merry;
The sun does descend,
And our sports have an end.

Round the laps of their mothers   25
Many sisters and brothers,
Like birds in their nest,
Are ready for rest,
And sport no more seen
On the darkening Green.   30

The Little Black Boy

My mother bore me in the southern wild,
And I am black, but O! my soul is white;
White as an angel is the English child,
But I am black, as if bereaved of light.

My mother taught me underneath a tree,   5
And, sitting down before the heat of day,
She took me on her lap and kissed me,
And, pointing to the east, began to say:

'Look on the rising sun,—there God does live,
And gives His light, and gives His heat away;   10
And flowers and trees and beasts and men receive
Comfort in morning, joy in the noonday.

'And we are put on earth a little space,
That we may learn to bear the beams of love;
And these black bodies and this sunburnt face   15
Is but a cloud, and like a shady grove.

'For when our souls have learned the heat to bear,
The cloud will vanish; we shall hear His voice,
Saying, "Come out from the grove, My love and care,
And round My golden tent like lambs rejoice." '   20

Thus did my mother say, and kissed me;
And thus I say to little English boy.
When I from black and he from white cloud free,
And round the tent of God like lambs we joy,

I'll shade him from the heat, till he can bear   25
To lean in joy upon our Father's knee;
And then I'll stand and stroke his silver hair,
And be like him, and he will then love me.

On Another's Sorrow

Can I see another's woe,
And not be in sorrow too?
Can I see another's grief,
And not seek for kind relief?

Can I see a falling tear,   5
And not feel my sorrow's share?
Can a father see his child
Weep, nor be with sorrow filled?

Can a mother sit and hear
An infant groan, an infant fear?   10
No, no! never can it be!
Never, never can it be!

And can He who smiles on all
Hear the wren with sorrows small,
Hear the small bird's grief and care,   15
Hear the woes that infants bear,

And not sit beside the nest,
Pouring pity in their breast;
And not sit the cradle near,
Weeping tear on infant's tear;   20

And not sit both night and day,
Wiping all our tears away?
O, no! never can it be!
Never, never can it be!

He doth give His joy to all;   25
He becomes an infant small;
He becomes a man of woe;
He doth feel the sorrow too.

Think not thou canst sigh a sigh,
And thy Maker is not by;   30
Think not thou canst weep a tear
And thy Maker is not near.

O! He gives to us His joy
That our grief He may destroy;
Till our grief is fled and gone   35
He doth sit by us and moan.

Night

The sun descending in the west,
The evening star does shine;
The birds are silent in their nest,
And I must seek for mine.
The moon, like a flower,   5
In heaven's high bower,
With silent delight
Sits and smiles on the night.

Farewell, green fields and happy groves,
Where flocks have took delight.   10
Where lambs have nibbled, silent moves
The feet of angels bright;
Unseen they pour blessing,
And joy without ceasing,
On each bud and blossom,   15
And each sleeping bosom.

They look in every thoughtless nest.
Where birds are covered warm;
They visit caves of every beast,
To keep them all from harm.   20
If they see any weeping
That should have been sleeping,
They pour sleep on their head,
And sit down by their bed.

When wolves and tigers how for prey,   25
They pitying stand and weep;
Seeking to drive their thirst away,
And keep them from the sheep.
But if they rush dreadful,
The angels, most heedful,   30
Receive each mild spirit,
New worlds to inherit.

And there the lion's ruddy eyes
Shall flow with tears of gold,
And pitying the tender cries,   35
And walking round the fold,
Saying 'Wrath, by His meekness,
And, by His health, sickness
Is driven away
From our immortal day.   40

'And now beside thee, bleating lamb,
I can lie down and sleep;
Or think on Him who bore thy name,
Graze after thee and weep.
For, washed in life's river,   45
My bright mane for ever
Shall shine like the gold
As I guard o'er the fold.'

The Little Girl Lost

In futurity
I prophetic see
That the earth from sleep
(Grave the sentence deep)

Shall arise and seek   5
For her Maker meek;
And the desert wild
Become a garden mild.

In the southern clime,
Where the summer's prime   10
Never fades away,
Lovely Lyca lay.

Seven summers old
Lovely Lyca told;
She had wandered long   15
Hearing wild birds' song.

'Sweet sleep, come to me
Underneath this tree.
Do father, mother weep?
Where can Lyca sleep?   20

'Lost in desert wild
Is your little child.
How can Lyca sleep
If her mother weep?

43

'If her heart does ache   25
Then let Lyca wake;
If my mother sleep,
Lyca shall not weep.

'Frowning, frowning night,
O'er this desert bright,   30
Let thy moon arise
While I close my eyes.'

Sleeping Lyca lay
While the beasts of prey,
Come from caverns deep,   35
Viewed the maid asleep.

The kingly lion stood,
And the virgin viewed,
Then he gambolled round
O'er the hallowed ground.   40

Leopards, tigers play
Round her as she lay,
While the lion old
Bowed his mane of gold,

And her bosom lick,   45
And upon her neck
From his eyes of flame
Ruby tears there came;

While the lioness
Loosed her slender dress,   50
And naked they conveyed
To caves the sleeping maid.

The Little Girl Found

All the night in woe
Lyca's parents go
Over valleys deep,
While the deserts weep.

Tired and woe-begone,   5
Hoarse with making moan,
Arm in arm seven days
They traced the desert ways.

Seven nights they sleep
Among shadows deep,   10
And dream they see their child
Starved in desert wild.

Pale, thro' pathless ways
The fancied image strays
Famished, weeping, weak,   15
With hollow piteous shriek.

Rising from unrest,
The trembling woman pressed
With feet of weary woe:
She could no further go.   20

In his arms he bore
Her, armed with sorrow sore;
Till before their way
A couching lion lay.

45

Turning back was vain: 25
Soon his heavy mane
Bore them to the ground.
Then he stalked around,

Smelling to his prey;
But their fears allay   30
When he licks their hands,
And silent by them stands.

They look upon his eyes
Filled with deep surprise;
And wondering behold   35
A spirit armed in gold.

On his head a crown;
On his shoulders down
Flowed his golden hair.
Gone was all their care.   40

'Follow me,' he said;
'Weep not for the maid;
In my palace deep
Lyca lies asleep.'

Then they follow èd   45
Where the vision led,
And saw their sleeping child
Among tigers wild.

To this day they dwell
In a lonely dell;   50
Nor fear the wolfish howl
Nor the lions' growl.

The Schoolboy

I love to rise in a summer morn
When the birds sing on every tree;
The distant huntsman winds his horn,
And the skylark sings with me.
O! what sweet company!   5

But to go to school in a summer morn,
O! it drives all joy away;
Under a cruel eye outworn,
The little ones spend the day
In sighing and dismay.   10

Ah! then at times I drooping sit,
And spend many an anxious hour,
Nor in my book can I take delight,
Nor sit in learning's bower,
Worn thro' with the dreary shower.   15

How can the bird that is born for joy
Sit in a cage and sing?
How can a child, when fears annoy,
But droop his tender wing,
And forget his youthful spring?   20

O! father and mother, if buds are nipped
And blossoms blown away,
And if the tender plants are stripped
Of their joy in the springing day,
By sorrow and care's dismay,   25

47

How shall the summer arise in joy,
Or the summer fruits appear?
Or how shall we gather what griefs destroy,
Or bless the mellowing year,
When the blasts of winter appear? 30

The Voice of the Ancient Bard

Youth of delight, come hither,
And see the opening morn,
Image of truth new-born.
Doubt is fled, and clouds of reason,
Dark disputes and artful teasing. 5
Folly is an endless maze,
Tangled roots perplex her ways.
How many have fallen there!
They stumble all night over bones of the dead,
And feel they know not what but care, 10
And wish to lead others, when they should be led.

My Pretty Rose-tree

A flower was offered to me,
Such a flower as May never bore;
But I said, 'I've a pretty Rose-tree,'
And I passed the sweet flower o'er.

Then I went to my pretty Rose-tree, 5
To tend her by day and by night,
But my Rose turned away with jealousy,
And her thorns were my only delight.

'Never seek to tell thy love'

Never seek to tell thy love,
Love that never told can be;
For the gentle wind does move
Silently, invisibly.

I told my love, I told my love,   5
I told her all my heart;
Trembling, cold, in ghastly fears,
Ah! she doth depart.

Soon as she was gone from me,
A traveller came by,   10
Silently, invisibly:
He took her with a sigh.

The Clod and the Pebble

'Love seeketh not itself to please,
Nor for itself hath any care,
But for another gives its ease,
And builds a Heaven in Hell's despair.'

So sung a little Clod of Clay,   5
Trodden with the cattle's feet;
But a Pebble of the brook
Warbled out these metres meet:

'Love seeketh only self to please,
To bind another to its delight,   10
Joys in another's loss of ease,
And builds a Hell in Heaven's despite.'

49

'I laid me down upon a bank'

I laid me down upon a bank,
Where Love lay sleeping;
I heard among the rushes dank
Weeping, weeping.

Then I went to the heath and the wild,   5
To the thistles and thorns of the waste;
And they told me how they were beguiled,
Driven out, and compelled to be chaste.

The Garden of Love

I went to the Garden of Love,
And saw what I never had seen:
A Chapel was built in the midst,
Where I used to play on the green.

And the gates of this Chapel were shut,   5
And 'Thou shalt not' writ over the door;
So I turned to the Garden of Love
That so many sweet flowers bore;

And I saw it was filled with graves,
And tomb-stones where flowers should be;   10
And priests in black gowns were walking their rounds,
And binding with briars my joys and desires.

'I saw a Chapel all of gold'

I saw a Chapel all of gold
That none did dare to enter in,
And many weeping stood without,
Weeping, mourning, worshipping.

I saw a Serpent rise between   5
The white pillars of the door,
And he forced and forced and forced;
Down the golden hinges tore,

And along the pavement sweet,
Set with pearls and rubies bright,   10
All his slimy length he drew,
Till upon the altar white

Vomiting his poison out
On the Bread and on the Wine.
So I turned into a sty,   15
And laid me down among the swine.

'I asked a thief to steal me a peach'

I asked a thief to steal me a peach:
He turned up his eyes.
I asked a lithe lady to lie her down:
Holy and meek, she cries.

As soon as I went   5
An Angel came:
He winked at the thief,
And smiled at the dame;

And without one word said
Had a peach from the tree,   10
And still as a maid
Enjoyed the lady.

' I heard an Angel singing '

I heard an Angel singing
When the day was springing:
'Mercy, Pity, Peace
Is the world's release.'

Thus he sung all day   5
Over the new-mown hay,
Till the sun went down,
And haycocks looked brown.

I heard a Devil curse
Over the heath and the furze: 10
'Mercy could be no more
If there was nobody poor,

'And Pity no more could be,
If all were as happy as we.'
At his curse the sun went down,   15
And the heavens gave a frown.

Down poured the heavy rain
Over the new-reaped grain;
And Misery's increase
Is Mercy, Pity, Peace.   20

A Poison Tree

I was angry with my friend:
I told my wrath, my wrath did end.
I was angry with my foe:
I told it not, my wrath did grow.

And I watered it in fears,   5
Night and morning with my tears;
And I sunned it with smiles,
And with soft deceitful wiles.

And it grew both day and night.
Till it bore an apple bright;   10
And my foe beheld it shine,
And he knew that it was mine,

And into my garden stole
When the night had veiled the pole:
In the morning glad I see   15
My foe outstretched beneath the tree.

'I feared the fury of my wind'

I feared the fury of my wind
Would blight all blossoms fair and true;
And my sun it shined and shined,
And my wind it never blew.

But a blossom fair or true   5
Was not found on any tree;
For all blossoms grew and grew
Fruitless, false, tho' fair to see.

'Why should I care for the men of Thames'

Why should I care for the men of Thames,
Or the cheating waves of chartered streams;
Or shrink at the little blasts of fear
That the hireling blows into my ear?

Tho' born on the cheating banks of Thames,   5
Tho' his waters bathed my infant limbs,
The Ohio shall wash his stains from me:
I was born a slave, but I go to be free!

'Silent, silent night'

Silent, silent Night,
Quench the holy light
Of thy torches bright;

For possessed of Day
Thousand spirits stray   5
That sweet joys betray.

Why should joys be sweet
Used with deceit,
Nor with sorrows meet?

But an honest joy   10
Does itself destroy
For a harlot coy.

'O lapwing! thou flyest around the heath'

O Lapwing! thou flyest around the heath,
Nor seest the net that is spread beneath.
Why dost thou not fly among the corn fields?
They cannot spread nets where a harvest yields.

In a Myrtle Shade

Why should I be bound to thee,
O my lovely Myrtle-tree?
Love, free Love, cannot be bound
To any tree that grows on ground.

O! how sick and weary I   5
Underneath my Myrtle lie;
Like to dung upon the ground,
Underneath my Myrtle bound.

Oft my Myrtle sighed in vain
To behold my heavy chain: 10
Oft my Father saw us sigh,
And laughed at our simplicity.

So I smote him, and his gore
Stained the roots my Myrtle bore.
But the time of youth is fled,   15
And grey hairs are on my head.

London

I wander thro' each chartered street,
Near where the chartered Thames does flow,
And mark in every face I meet
Marks of weakness, marks of woe.

In every cry of every man,   5
In every infant's cry of fear,
In every voice, in every ban
The mind-forged manacles I hear.

How the chimney-sweeper's cry
Every blackening church appals;   10
And the hapless soldier's sigh
Runs in blood down palace walls.

But most thro' midnight streets I hear
How the youthful harlot's curse
Blasts the new-born infant's tear,   15
And blights with plagues the marriage hearse.

To Nobodaddy

Why art thou silent and invisible,
Father of Jealousy?
Why dost thou hide thyself in clouds
From every searching eye?

Why darkness and obscurity   5
In all thy words and laws,
That none dare eat the fruit but from
The wily Serpent's jaws?
Or is it because secrecy gains females' loud applause?

The Lily

The modest Rose puts forth a thorn,
The humble Sheep a threatening horn;
While the Lily white shall in love delight,
Nor a thorn, nor a threat stain her beauty bright.

'Are not the joys of morning sweeter'

Are not the joys of morning sweeter
Than the joys of night?
And are the vigorous joys of youth
Ashamed of the light?

Let age and sickness silent rob
The vineyards in the night;
But those who burn with vigorous youth
Pluck fruits before the light.

The Wild Flower's Song

As I wandered the forest,
The green leaves among,
I heard a Wild Flower
Singing a song.

'I slept in the earth
In the silent night,
I murmured my fears
And I felt delight.

'In the morning I went,
As rosy as morn,
To seek for new joy;
But, oh! met with scorn.'

To My Myrtle

To a lovely Myrtle bound,
Blossoms showering all around,
O! how sick and weary I
Underneath my Myrtle lie!
Why should I be bound to thee,
O my lovely Myrtle-tree?

The Little Vagabond

Dear mother, dear mother, the Church is cold,
But the Ale-house is healthy and pleasant and warm;
Besides I can tell where I am used well,
Such usage in Heaven will never do well.

But if at the Church they would give us some ale,   5
And a pleasant fire our souls to regale,
We'd sing and we'd pray all the livelong day,
Nor ever once wish from the Church to stray.

Then the Parson might preach, and drink, and sing,
And we'd be as happy as birds in the spring;   10
And modest Dame Lurch, who is always at church,
Would not have bandy children, nor fasting, nor birch.

And God, like a father, rejoicing to see
His children as pleasant and happy as He,
Would have no more quarrel with the Devil or the barrel, 15
But kiss him, and give him both drink and apparel.

The Fly

Little Fly,
Thy summer's play
My thoughtless hand
Has brushed away.

Am not I   5
A fly like thee?
Or art not thou
A man like me?

For I dance,
And drink, and sing,   10
Till some blind hand
Shall brush my wing.

If thought is life
And strength and breath,
And the want   15
Of thought is death,

Then am I
A happy fly,
If I live
Or if I die.   20

A Little Girl Lost

Children of the future age,
Reading this indignant page,
Know that in a former time,
Love, sweet Love, was thought a crime!

In the Age of Gold,   5
Free from winter's cold,
Youth and maiden bright
To the holy light,
Naked in the sunny beams delight

Once a youthful pair,   10
Filled with softest care,
Met in garden bright
Where the holy light
Had just removed the curtains of the night.

There, in rising day,   15
On the grass they play;
Parents were afar,
Strangers came not near,
And the maiden soon forgot her fear.

Tired with kisses sweet,   20
They agree to meet
When the silent sleep
Waves o'er heaven's deep,
And the weary tired wanderers weep.

To her father white   25
Came the maiden bright;
But his loving look,
Like the holy book,
All her tender limbs with terror shook.

'Ona! pale and weak!   30
To thy father speak:
O! the trembling fear,
O! the dismal care,
That shakes the blossoms of my hoary hair!'

Ah! Sun-flower

Ah! Sun-flower, weary of time,
Who countest the steps of the sun;
Seeking after that sweet golden clime,
Where the traveller's journey is done;

Where the Youth pined away with desire,
And the pale Virgin shrouded in snow,
Arise from their graves, and aspire
Where my Sun-flower wishes to go.

To Tirzah

Whate'er is born of mortal birth
Must be consumed with the earth,
To rise from generation free:
Then what have I to do with thee?

The sexes sprung from shame and pride,
Blowed in the morn, in evening died;
But Mercy changed death into sleep;
The sexes rose to work and weep.

Thou, mother of my mortal part,
With cruelty didst mould my heart,
And with false self-deceiving tears
Didst bind my nostrils, eyes, and ears;

Didst close my tongue in senseless clay,
And me to mortal life betray:
The death of Jesus set me free:
Then what have I to do with thee?

EXTRACTS FROM
THE MARRIAGE OF HEAVEN AND HELL

The Argument

Rintrah roars, and shakes his fires in the burdened air;
Hungry clouds swag on the deep.

Once meek, and in a perilous path,
The just man kept his course along
The vale of death.   5
Roses are planted where thorns grow,
And on the barren heath
Sing the honey bees.

Then the perilous path was planted,
And a river and a spring   10
On every cliff and tomb,
And on the bleached bones
Red clay brought forth;

Till the villain left the paths of ease,
To walk in perilous paths, and drive   15
The just man into barren climes.

Now the sneaking serpent walks
In mild humility,
And the just man rages in the wilds
Where lions roam.   20

Rintrah roars, and shakes his fires in the burdened air;
Hungry clouds swag on the deep.

As a new heaven is begun, and it is now thirty-three years since its advent, the Eternal Hell revives. And lo! Swedenborg is the Angel sitting at the tomb: his writings are the linen clothes folded up. Now is the dominion of Edom, and the return of Adam into Paradise. See Isaiah xxxiv and xxxv chap.

Without Contraries is no progression. Attraction and Repulsion, Reason and Energy, Love and Hate, are necessary to Human existence.

From these contraries spring what the religious call Good and Evil. Good is the passive that obeys Reason. Evil is the active springing from Energy.

Good is Heaven. Evil is Hell.

The Voice of the Devil

All Bibles or sacred codes have been the causes of the following Errors:—

1. That Man has two real existing principles, viz. a Body and a Soul.

2. That Energy, called Evil, is alone from the Body; and that Reason, called Good, is alone from the Soul.

3. That God will torment Man in Eternity for following his Energies.

But the following Contraries to these are True:—

1. Man has no Body distinct from his Soul; for that called Body is a portion of Soul discerned by the five Senses, the chief inlets of Soul in this age.

2. Energy is the only life, and is from the Body; and Reason is the bound or outward circumference of Energy.

3. Energy is Eternal Delight.

Those who restrain Desire, do so because theirs is weak enough to be restrained; and the restrainer or Reason usurps its place and governs the unwilling.

And being restrained, it by degrees becomes passive, till it is only the shadow of Desire.

The history of this is written in *Paradise Lost*, and the Governor or Reason is called Messiah.

And the original Archangel, or possessor of the command of the Heavenly Host, is called the Devil or Satan, and his children are called Sin and Death.

But in the Book of Job, Milton's Messiah is called Satan.

For this history has been adopted by both parties.

It indeed appeared to Reason as if Desire was cast out; but the Devil's account is that the Messiah fell and formed a Heaven of what he stole from the Abyss.

This is shown in the Gospel, where he prays to the Father to send the Comforter, or Desire, that Reason may have Ideas to build on; the Jehovah of the Bible being no other than he who dwells in flaming fire.

Know that after Christ's death he became Jehovah.

But in Milton, the Father is Destiny, the Son a Ratio of the five senses, and the Holy Ghost Vacuum!

Note. The reason Milton wrote in fetters when he wrote of Angels and God, and at liberty when of Devils and Hell, is because he was a true Poet, and of the Devil's party without knowing it.

A Memorable Fancy

As I was walking among the fires of Hell, delighted with the enjoyments of Genius, which to Angels look like torment and insanity, I collected some of their Proverbs; thinking that as the sayings used in a nation mark its character, so the Proverbs of

Hell show the nature of Infernal wisdom better than any description of buildings or garments.

When I came home, on the abyss of the five senses, where a flat-sided steep frowns over the present world, I saw a mighty Devil, folded in black clouds, hovering on the sides of the rock: with corroding fires he wrote the following sentence now perceived by the minds of men, and read by them on earth:—

> How do you know but every Bird that cuts the airy way
> Is an immense World of Delight, closed by your senses five?

Proverbs of Hell

In seed time learn, in harvest teach, in winter enjoy.
Drive your cart and your plough over the bones of the dead.
The road of excess leads to the palace of wisdom.
Prudence is a rich, ugly old maid courted by Incapacity.
He who desires but acts not, breeds pestilence.
The cut worm forgives the plough.
Dip him in the river who loves water.
A fool sees not the same tree that a wise man sees.
He whose face gives no light, shall never become a star.
Eternity is in love with the productions of time.
The busy bee has no time for sorrow.
The hours of folly are measured by the clock; but of wisdom, no clock can measure.
All wholesome food is caught without a net or a trap.
Bring out number, weight, and measure in a year of dearth.
No bird soars too high, if he soars with his own wings.
A dead body revenges not injuries.
The most sublime act is to set another before you.
If the fool would persist in his folly he would become wise.
Folly is the cloak of knavery.

Shame is Pride's cloak.

Prisons are built with stones of Law, brothels with bricks of Religion.

The pride of the peacock is the glory of God.

The lust of the goat is the bounty of God.

The wrath of the lion is the wisdom of God.

The nakedness of woman is the work of God.

Excess of sorrow laughs. Excess of joy weeps.

The roaring of lions, the howling of wolves, the raging of the stormy sea, and the destructive sword are portions of eternity too great for the eye of man.

The fox condemns the trap, not himself.

Joys impregnate. Sorrows bring forth.

Let man wear the fell of the lion, woman the fleece of the sheep.

The bird a nest, the spider a web, man friendship.

The selfish, smiling fool, and the sullen, frowning fool shall be both thought wise, that they may be a rod.

What is now proved was once only imagined.

The rat, the mouse, the fox, the rabbit watch the roots; the lion, the tiger, the horse, the elephant watch the fruits.

The cistern contains: the fountain overflows.

One thought fills immensity.

Always be ready to speak your mind, and a base man will avoid you.

Everything possible to be believed is an image of truth.

The eagle never lost so much time as when he submitted to learn of the crow.

The fox provides for himself; but God provides for the lion.

Think in the morning. Act in the noon. Eat in the evening. Sleep in the night.

He who has suffered you to impose on him, knows you.

As the plough follows words, so God rewards prayers.

The tigers of wrath are wiser than the horses of instruction

Expect poison from the standing water.

67

You never know what is enough unless you know what is more than enough.

Listen to the fool's reproach! it is a kingly title!

The eyes of fire, the nostrils of air, the mouth of water, the beard of earth.

The weak in courage is strong in cunning.

The apple tree never asks the beech how he shall grow; nor the lion the horse how he shall take his prey.

The thankful receiver bears a plentiful harvest.

If others had not been foolish, we should be so.

The soul of sweet delight can never be defiled.

When thou seest an eagle, thou seest a portion of Genius; lift up thy head!

As the caterpillar chooses the fairest leaves to lay her eggs on, so the priest lays his curse on the fairest joys.

To create a little flower is the labour of ages.

Damn braces. Bless relaxes.

The best wine is the oldest, the best water the newest.

Prayers plough not! Praises reap not!

Joys laugh not! Sorrows weep not!

The head Sublime, the heart Pathos, the genitals Beauty, the hands and feet Proportion.

As the air to a bird or the sea to a fish, so is contempt to the contemptible.

The crow wished everything was black, the owl that everything was white.

Exuberance is Beauty.

If the lion was advised by the fox, he would be cunning.

Improvement makes straight roads; but the crooked roads without improvement are roads of Genius.

Sooner murder an infant in its cradle than nurse unacted desires.

Where man is not, nature is barren.

Truth can never be told so as to be understood and not be believed.

Enough, or Too much.

The ancient Poets animated all sensible objects with Gods or Geniuses, calling them by the names and adorning them with the properties of woods, rivers, mountains, lakes, cities, nations, and whatever their enlarged and numerous senses could perceive.

And particularly they studied the Genius of each city and country, placing it under its Mental Deity;

Till a System was formed, which some took advantage of and enslaved the vulgar by attempting to realize or abstract the Mental Deities from their objects—thus began Priesthood;

Choosing forms of worship from poetic tales.

And at length they pronounced that the Gods had ordered such things.

Thus men forgot that All Deities reside in the Human breast.

A Song of Liberty

1. The Eternal Female groaned! It was heard over all the Earth.
2. Albion's coast is sick, silent. The American meadows faint!
3. Shadows of Prophecy shiver along by the lakes and the rivers, and mutter across the ocean. France, rend down thy dungeon!
4. Golden Spain, burst the barriers of old Rome!
5. Cast thy keys, O Rome! into the deep, down falling, even to eternity down falling,
6. And weep.
7. In her trembling hands she took the new-born terror, howling.
8. On those infinite mountains of light, now barred out by the Atlantic sea, the new-born fire stood before the starry king!
9. Flagged with grey-browed snows and thunderous visages, the jealous wings waved over the deep.
10. The speary hand burned aloft, unbuckled was the shield; forth went the hand of Jealousy among the flaming hair, and hurled the new-born wonder thro' the starry night.

11. The fire, the fire, is falling!

12. Look up! look up! O citizen of London, enlarge thy countenance! O Jew, leave counting gold! return to thy oil and wine. O African! black African! Go, wingèd thought, widen his forehead!

13. The fiery limbs, the flaming hair, shot like the sinking sun into the western sea.

14. Waked from his eternal sleep, the hoary element, roaring, fled away.

15. Down rushed, beating his wings in vain, the jealous King; his grey-browed counsellors, thunderous warriors, curled veterans, among helms, and shields, and chariots, horses, elephants, banners, castles, slings, and rocks,

16. Falling, rushing, ruining! buried in the ruins, on Urthona's dens;

17. All night beneath the ruins; then, their sullen flames faded, emerge round the gloomy King.

18. With thunder and fire, leading his starry hosts thro' the waste wilderness, he promulgates his ten commands, glancing his beamy eyelids over the deep in dark dismay,

19. Where the son of fire in his eastern cloud, while the morning plumes her golden breast,

20. Spurning the clouds written with curses, stamps the stony law to dust, loosing the eternal horses from the dens of night, crying: *Empire is no more! and now the lion and wolf shall cease.*

Chorus

Let the Priests of the Raven of dawn no longer, in deadly black, with hoarse note curse the suns of joy! Nor his accepted brethren—whom, tyrant, he calls free—lay the bound or build the roof! Nor pale Religious lechery call that Virginity that wishes but acts not!

For everything that lives is Holy!

SELECTION OF LATER LYRICS

'And did those feet in ancient time'

And did those feet in ancient time
　　Walk upon England's mountains green?
And was the holy Lamb of God
　　On England's pleasant pastures seen?

And did the Countenance Divine　　　　　　5
　　Shine forth upon our clouded hills?
And was Jerusalem builded here
　　Among these dark Satanic Mills?

Bring me my bow of burning gold!
　　Bring me my arrows of desire!　　　　　10
Bring me my spear! O clouds, unfold!
　　Bring me my chariot of fire!

I will not cease from mental fight,
　　Nor shall my sword sleep in my hand,
Till we have built Jerusalem　　　　　　　15
　　In England's green and pleasant land.

'The fields from Islington to Marylebone'

The fields from Islington to Marylebone,
　　To Primrose Hill and Saint John's Wood,
Were builded over with pillars of gold;
　　And there Jerusalem's pillars stood.

Her Little Ones ran on the fields,
   The Lamb of God among them seen,
And fair Jerusalem, His Bride,
   Among the little meadows green.

Pancras and Kentish Town repose
   Among her golden pillars high,
Among her golden arches which
   Shine upon the starry sky.

The Jew's-harp House and the Green Man,
   The ponds where boys to bathe delight,
The fields of cows by Willan's farm,
   Shine in Jerusalem's pleasant sight.

She walks upon our meadows green;
   The Lamb of God walks by her side;
And every English child is seen,
   Children of Jesus and His Bride;

Forgiving trespasses and sins,
   Lest Babylon, with cruel Og,
With moral and self-righteous Law,
   Should crucify in Satan's Synagogue.

What are those Golden Builders doing
   Near mournful ever-weeping Paddington,
Standing above that mighty ruin,
   Where Satan the first victory won;

Where Albion slept beneath the fatal Tree,
   And the Druids' golden knife
Rioted in human gore,
   In offerings of human life?

They groaned aloud on London Stone,
   They groaned aloud on Tyburn's Brook:
Albion gave his deadly groan,   35
   And all the Atlantic mountains shook.

Albion's Spectre, from his loins,
   Tore forth in all the pomp of war;
Satan his name; in flames of fire
   He stretched his Druid pillars far.   40

Jerusalem fell from Lambeth's vale,
   Down thro' Poplar and Old Bow,
Thro' Malden, and across the sea,
   In war and howling, death and woe.

The Rhine was red with human blood;   45
   The Danube rolled a purple tide;
On the Euphrates Satan stood,
   And over Asia stretched his pride.

He withered up sweet Zion's hill
   From every nation of the Earth;   50
He withered up Jerusalem's Gates,
   And in a dark land gave her birth.

He withered up the Human Form
   By laws of sacrifice for Sin,
Till it became a Mortal Worm,   55
   But O! translucent all within.

The Divine Vision still was seen,
   Still was the Human Form Divine;
Weeping, in weak and mortal clay,
   O Jesus! still the Form was Thine!   60

And Thine the Human Face; and Thine
   The Human Hands, and Feet, and Breath,
Entering thro' the Gates of Birth,
   And passing thro' the Gates of Death.

And O Thou Lamb of God! whom I   65
   Slew in my dark self-righteous pride,
Art Thou returned to Albion's land,
   And is Jerusalem Thy Bride?

Come to my arms, and nevermore
   Depart; but dwell for ever here;   70
Create my spirit to Thy love;
   Subdue my Spectre to Thy fear.

Spectre of Albion! warlike Fiend!
   In clouds of blood and ruin rolled,
I here reclaim thee as my own,   75
   My Selfhood—Satan armed in gold!

Is this thy soft family-love,
   Thy cruel patriarchal pride;
Planting thy family alone,
   Destroying all the world beside?   80

A man's worst enemies are those
   Of his own house and family;
And he who makes his Law a curse,
   By his own Law shall surely die!

In my Exchanges every land   85
   Shall walk; and mine in every land
Mutual shall build Jerusalem,
   Both heart in heart and hand in hand.

'England! awake! awake! awake!'

England! awake! awake! awake!
   Jerusalem thy sister calls!
Why wilt thou sleep the sleep of death,
   And close her from thy ancient walls?

Thy hills and valleys felt her feet   5
   Gently upon their bosoms move:
Thy gates beheld sweet Zion's ways;
   Then was a time of joy and love.

And now the time returns again:
   Our souls exult, and London's towers   10
Receive the Lamb of God to dwell
   In England's green and pleasant bowers.

The Golden Net

Three Virgins at the break of day:—
'Whither, young man, whither away?
Alas for woe! alas for woe!'
They cry, and tears for ever flow.
The one was clothed in flames of fire,   5
The other clothed in iron wire,
The other clothed in tears and sighs
Dazzling bright before my eyes.
They bore a Net of golden twine
To hang upon the branches fine.   10

Pitying I wept to see the woe
That Love and Beauty undergo,
To be consumed in burning fires
And in ungratified desires,
And in tears clothed night and day   15
Melted all my soul away.
When they saw my tears, a smile
That did Heaven itself beguile,
Bore the Golden Net aloft,
As on downy pinions soft,   20
Over the morning of my day.
Underneath the Net I stray,
Now entreating burning Fire
Now entreating Iron Wire,
Now entreating Tears and Sighs—   25
O! when will the morning rise?

The Mental Traveller

I travelled thro' a land of men,
A land of men and women too;
And heard and saw such dreadful things
As cold earth-wanderers never knew.

For there the Babe is born in joy   5
That was begotten in dire woe;
Just as we reap in joy the fruit
Which we in bitter tears did sow.

And if the Babe is born a boy
He's given to a Woman Old,   10
Who nails him down upon a rock,
Catches his shrieks in cups of gold.

She binds iron thorns around his head,
She pierces both his hands and feet,
She cuts his heart out at his side,   15
To make it feel both cold and heat.

Her fingers number every nerve,
Just as a miser counts his gold;
She lives upon his shrieks and cries,
And she grows young as he grows old.   20

Till he becomes a bleeding Youth,
And she becomes a Virgin bright;
Then he rends up his manacles,
And binds her down for his delight.

He plants himself in all her nerves,   25
Just as a husbandman his mould;
And she becomes his dwelling-place
And garden fruitful seventyfold.

An aged shadow, soon he fades,
Wandering round an earthly cot,   30
Full filled all with gems and gold
Which he by industry had got.

And these are the gems of the human soul,
The rubies and pearls of a love-sick eye,
The countless gold of the aching heart,   35
The martyr's groan and the lover's sigh.

They are his meat, they are his drink;
He feeds the beggar and the poor
And the wayfaring traveller:
For ever open is his door.   40

His grief is their eternal joy;
They make the roofs and walls to ring;
Till from the fire on the hearth
A little female Babe does spring.

And she is all of solid fire   45
And gems and gold, that none his hand
Dares stretch to touch her baby form,
Or wrap her in his swaddling-band.

But she comes to the man she loves,
If young or old, or rich or poor;   50
They soon drive out the aged host,
A beggar at another's door.

He wanders weeping far away,
Until some other take him in;
Oft blind and age-bent, sore distrest,   55
Until he can a Maiden win.

And to allay his freezing age,
The poor man takes her in his arms;
The cottage fades before his sight,
The garden and its lovely charms.   60

The guests are scattered thro' the land,
For the eye altering alters all;
The senses roll themselves in fear,
And the flat earth becomes a ball;

The stars, sun, moon, all shrink away, 65
A desert vast without a bound,
And nothing left to eat or drink,
And a dark desert all around

The honey of her infant lips,
The bread and wine of her sweet smile,   70
The wild game of her roving eye,
Does him to infancy beguile;

For as he eats and drinks he grows
Younger and younger every day;
And on the desert wild they both   75
Wander in terror and dismay.

Like the wild stag she flees away,
Her fear plants many a thicket wild;
While he pursues her night and day,
By various arts of love beguiled;   80

By various arts of love and hate,
Till the wide desert's planted o'er
With labyrinths of wayward love,
Where roam the lion, wolf, and boar;

Till he becomes a wayward Babe,   85
And she a weeping Woman Old.
Then many a lover wanders here;
The sun and stars are nearer rolled;

The trees bring forth sweet ecstasy
To all who in the desert roam;   90
Till many a city there is built,
And many a pleasant shepherd's home.

But when they find the frowning Babe,
Terror strikes thro' the region wide:
They cry 'The Babe! the Babe is born!'   95
And flee away on every side.

For who dare touch the Frowning Form,
His arm is withered to its root;
Lions, boars, wolves, all howling flee,
And every tree does shed its fruit.   100

And none can touch that frowning form,
Except it be a Woman Old;
She nails him down upon the rock.
And all is done as I have told.

The Crystal Cabinet

The Maiden caught me in the wild,
Where I was dancing merrily;
She put me into her Cabinet,
And locked me up with a golden key.

This Cabinet is formed of gold   5
And pearl and crystal shining bright,
And within it opens into a world
And a little lovely moony night.

Another England there I saw,
Another London with its Tower,   10
Another Thames and other hills,
And another pleasant Surrey bower,

Another Maiden like herself,
Translucent, lovely, shining clear,
Threefold each in the other closed—   15
O, what a pleasant trembling fear!

O, what a smile! a threefold smile
Filled me, that like a flame I burned;
I bent to kiss the lovely Maid,
And found a threefold kiss returned.   20

I strove to seize the inmost form
With ardour fierce and hands of flame,
But burst the Crystal Cabinet,
And like a weeping Babe became—

A weeping Babe upon the wild,   25
And weeping Woman pale reclined,
And in the outward air again
I filled with woes the passing wind.

Auguries of Innocence

To see a World in a grain of sand,
And a Heaven in a wild flower,
Hold Infinity in the palm of your hand,
And Eternity in an hour.
A robin redbreast in a cage   5
Puts all Heaven in a rage. . . .
Each outcry of the hunted hare
A fibre from the brain does tear.
A skylark wounded in the wing,
A cherubim does cease to sing. . . .   10
Every wolf's and lion's howl
Raises from Hell a human soul.
The wild deer, wandering here and there,
Keeps the human soul from care.

The lamb misused breeds public strife, 15
And yet forgives the butcher's knife. . . .
It is right it should be so;
Man was made for joy and woe;
And when this we rightly know,
Thro' the world we safely go. 20
Joy and woe are woven fine,
A clothing for the soul divine;
Under every grief and pine
Runs a joy with silken twine.
The babe is more than swaddling-bands; 25
Throughout all these human lands
Tools were made, and born were hands,
Every farmer understands. . . .
The emmet's inch and eagle's mile
Make lame philosophy to smile. 30
He who doubts from what he sees
Will ne'er believe, do what you please.
If the sun and moon should doubt,
They'd immediately go out.
To be in a passion you good may do, 35
But no good if a passion is in you.
The whore and gambler, by the state
Licensed, build that nation's fate.
The harlot's cry from street to street
Shall weave Old England's winding-sheet. 40
The winner's shout, the loser's curse,
Dance before dead England's hearse.
Every night and every morn
Some to misery are born.
Every morn and every night 45
Some are born to sweet delight.
Some are born to sweet delight,
Some are born to endless night. . . .

'Mock on, mock on, Voltaire, Rousseau'

Mock on, mock on, Voltaire, Rousseau;
Mock on, mock on; 'tis all in vain!
You throw the sand against the wind,
And the wind blows it back again.

And every sand becomes a gem   5
Reflected in the beams divine;
Blown back they blind the mocking eye,
But still in Israel's paths they shine.

The Atoms of Democritus
And Newton's Particles of Light   10
Are sands upon the Red Sea shore,
Where Israel's tents do shine so bright.

Morning

To find the Western path,
Right thro' the Gates of Wrath
I urge my way;
Sweet Mercy leads me on
With soft repentant moan: 5
I see the break of day.

The war of swords and spears,
Melted by dewy tears,
Exhales on high;
The Sun is freed from fears,   10
And with soft grateful tears
Ascends the sky.

The Everlasting Gospel

The vision of Christ that thou dost see
Is my vision's greatest enemy.
Thine has a great hook nose like thine;
Mine has a snub nose like to mine.
Thine is the Friend of all Mankind;   5
Mine speaks in parables to the blind.
Thine loves the same world that mine hates;
Thy heaven doors are my hell gates.
Socrates taught what Meletus
Loathed as a nation's bitterest curse,   10
And Caiaphas was in his own mind
A benefactor to mankind.
Both read the Bible day and night,
But thou read'st black where I read white. . . .

Was Jesus humble? or did He   15
Give any proofs of humility?
Boast of high things with humble tone,
And give with charity a stone?
When but a child He ran away,
And left His parents in dismay.   20
When they had wandered three days long
These were the words upon His tongue:
'No earthly parents I confess:
I am doing My Father's business.' . . .

Did Jesus teach doubt? or did He   25
Give any lessons of philosophy,

Charge visionaries with deceiving,
Or call men wise for not believing? . . .

Was Jesus born of a Virgin pure
With narrow soul and looks demure?   30
If He intended to take on sin
The Mother should an harlot been,
Just such a one as Magdalen,
With seven devils in her pen.
Or were Jew virgins still more cursed,   35
And more sucking devils nursed?
Or what was it which He took on
That He might bring salvation?
A body subject to be tempted,
From neither pain nor grief exempted;   40
Or such a body as might not feel
The passions that with sinners deal? . . .

Was Jesus chaste? or did He
Give any lessons of chastity?
The morning blushed fiery red: 45
Mary was found in adulterous bed;
Earth groaned beneath, and Heaven above
Trembled at discovery of Love. . . .

I am sure this Jesus will not do
Either for Englishman or Jew.   50

To the Accuser who is the God of this world

Truly, my Satan, thou art but a dunce,
And dost not know the garment from the man;
Every harlot was a virgin once,
Nor canst thou ever change Kate into Nan.

Tho' thou art worshipped by the names divine   5
Of Jesus and Jehovah, thou art still
The son of morn in weary night's decline,
The lost traveller's dream under the hill.

SELECTED APHORISMS
AND EPIGRAMS

'Love to faults is always blind'

Love to faults is always blind,
Always is to joy inclined,
Lawless, winged and unconfined,
And breaks all chains from every mind.

Deceit to secrecy confined,   5
Lawful, cautious and refined,
To anything but interest blind,
And forges fetters for the mind.

Soft Snow

I walked abroad in a snowy day:
I asked the soft Snow with me to play:
She played and she melted in all her prime;
And the Winter called it a dreadful crime.

'Abstinence sows sand all over'

Abstinence sows sand all over
The ruddy limbs and flaming hair,
But Desire gratified
Plants fruits of life and beauty there.

'He who binds to himself a joy'

He who binds to himself a Joy
Doth the wingèd life destroy;
But he who kisses the Joy as it flies
Lives in Eternity's sunrise.

The Question Answered

What is it men in women do require?
The lineaments of gratified desire.
What is it women do in men require?
The lineaments of gratified desire.

'When a man has married a wife,
he finds out whether'

When a man has married a wife, he finds out whether
Her knees and elbows are only glued together.

'Of H——'s birth this was the happy lot'

Of H——'s birth this was the happy lot:
His mother on his father him begot.

A petty sneaking knave I knew'

A petty sneaking knave I knew—
O! Mr. Cr——, how do ye do?

'Great things are done when men and mountains meet'

Great things are done when men and mountains meet;
This is not done by jostling in the street.

'The Angel that presided o'er my birth'

The Angel that presided o'er my birth
Said 'Little creature, formed of joy and mirth,
Gone love, without the help of anything on earth.'

NOTES

Preliminary Caution

Blake is one of the most difficult of the English poets, but the Victorian idea, still a popular one, that it is only the bad poems that are obscure is a vulgar error. With the exception of the early imitations and a few of the Songs of Innocence some degree of obscurity runs through *all* his poems, good, bad, and indifferent. There are three reasons why Blake's poetry is especially difficult—and why, therefore, it needs constant annotation:—

(1) He never went to school—Henry Pars's Drawing School was nothing but a drawing school—and so he missed the mental discipline, or perhaps distortion, involved in learning Latin, to which almost every other English poet has been subjected. And, because he never had to worry out the special problems that translation into and out of an inflected language raises for English speakers, his grammar is often weak or vague. Prepositions in particular are used so loosely that the specific sense intended has to be worked out from the surrounding context.

(2) Blake's poetic eye is rarely wholly on the perceptual objects that the titles of his poems might suggest he is writing about—roses, nurses, tigers, little boys and girls, Milton, Jerusalem. In the well-known marginal note on Wordsworth's *Influence of Natural Objects in calling forth and strengthening the Imagination in Boyhood and Early Youth* (one of the preliminary extracts from *The Prelude* that Wordsworth published in 1815) he wrote that, in contradistinction to Wordsworth, 'Natural objects always did and now do weaken, deaden or obliterate imagination in me'. Instead of the 'single vision' of eye-on-the-object poetry Blake cultivated what he called 'double vision'. The expository doggerel sent to Thomas Butts on November 22nd, 1802, gives two simple examples of this 'double vision'. One is a thistle encountered on a walk from Felpham to Lavant; outwardly a thistle but

> With my inward eye 'tis an old man grey.

And the thistle-old man is followed by a similar conjunction of the sun and Los, who represents the Spirit of Prophecy in Blake's mythological system:

'Twas outward a sun, inward Los in his might.

Unfortunately such expositions are rare in Blake and the 'inward' meanings of the symbols have to be reconstructed by the reader. This particular poem ends apocalyptically in threefold and fourfold vision ("Tis fourfold in my supreme delight'), for which he does *not* provide keys. By this date, however, Blake was deliberately cultivating a certain unintelligibility. 'Allegory,' he told Butts in a letter dated July 6th, 1803, 'addressed to the intellectual powers, while it is *altogether hidden* from the corporeal understanding, is my definition of the most sublime poetry' (my italics).

As a general guide to Blake's double vision the following list of the principal symbols should be useful to the beginner:

Innocence symbols (pre-sexual and amoral as well as Christian): children, sheep, wild birds, wild flowers, green fields, dawn, dew, spring—and associated images, e.g. shepherds, valleys, hills.

Energy symbols (creative, heroic, unrestrained—as well as revolutionary, righteously destructive): lions, tigers, wolves, eagles, noon, summer, sun, fire, forges, swords, spears, chariots. These overlap into:

Sexual symbols (from uninhibited ecstasy to selfish power over the beloved and jealousy): dreams, branches of trees, roses, gold, silver, moonlight—and associated images, e.g. nets, cages, fairies, bows and arrows. These overlap into:

Corruption symbols (hypocrisy, secrecy, as well as town-influences, including abstract reasoning): looms, curtains, cities, houses, snakes, evening, silence, disease. These overlap into:

Oppression symbols (personal, parental, religious, political): priests, mills, forests, mountains, seas, caves, clouds, thunder, frost, night, stars, winter, stone, iron.

Although it would be unwise to assume that the images in this list *always* carry the symbolic meanings indicated in every one of Blake's poems, they generally do. And the list is not by any means complete.

(3) Blake used his symbols—which are to be found even in some of the juvenilia in *Poetical Sketches*—to express increasingly subtle and complex intellectual distinctions. As the system developed, however, he found it necessary or convenient to reinforce the symbolism with an elaborate and cacophonous mythology that does not explain itself as the

symbols usually do. At the same time the symbols become increasingly esoteric and he introduces a technical vocabulary of his own. The north, for example, stands for reason, the south for desire, the east for wrath, and the west for pity. And the new key words such as *spectre*, *opaqueness*, *mundane shell*, *emanation* and the like are almost as unintelligible as Ulro, Golgonooza and Ololon. (They can be learnt by heart, but the non-professional reader resents having to do so.)

The total effect of these idiosyncrasies is to make Blake's English, especially after *c*. 1793–4, so personal that at times it almost becomes a private language. The modern reader's difficulty is that, if he is to enjoy and understand Blake's poetry *as poetry* (as distinct from psychology or philosophy), he cannot afford to allow the private language to intrude too far into it. The poems only exist as poems within the total context of English literature, i.e. as memorable statements written in the English language and controlled by the literary conventions that English poetry employs. No doubt there is always a certain tension between what a new poet wants to say and what the English language and literary tradition permit him to say, but this tension is more acute in Blake's case than in any other because of the extremity of his individualism. The stars, for example, cannot lose their normal connotation of brilliance, however much he tries to restrict their meaning to tyrannic power or abstract thought. The problem, then, for the reader of Blake (as it was for Blake himself) is to maintain a semantic balance between what Blake was trying to say and what the traditions of English speech and poetry were trying to make him say. It is perhaps in this no-man's-land of meaning, which is neither private nor public, that the Songs of Experience achieve their peculiar successes. But the balance was a difficult one to hold. In the lyrics of the Pickering MS. and the later Prophetic Books there are undeniable failures of communication. With patience a meaning is recoverable, but it is not exactly an English meaning. The reader must 'translate' Blake into English. In the special circumstances an editor can only provide the facts (both about Blake's private language, so far as that has been decoded, and about those aspects of the public poetic tradition that may not be generally known), arm the reader with this general caveat, and wish him *bon voyage*.

SELECTED LYRICS FROM *POETICAL SKETCHES*

Only twenty-two copies can now be traced of *Poetical Sketches. By W.B.* (1783), The book was printed privately, Anthony Stephen

Mathew, a London clergyman of culture and means, and John Flaxman the sculptor paying the printer's bill between them (it can only have been £6 or so), and there were probably not more than fifty copies altogether. A patronizing and not wholly accurate 'Advertisement' by Mathew is prefixed, which runs as follows:

> The following sketches were the production of untutored youth, commenced in his twelfth, and occasionally resumed by the author till his twentieth year; since which time, his talents having been wholly directed to the attainment of excellence in his profession, he has been deprived of the leisure requisite to such a revisal of these sheets, as might have rendered them less unfit to meet the public eye.
>
> Conscious of the irregularities and defects to be found in almost every page, his friends have still believed that they possessed a poetic originality, which merited some respite from oblivion. These their opinions remain, however, to be now reproved or confirmed by a less partial public.

Perhaps Mathew had hoped at this time to issue the book in the ordinary way through a bookseller. In the end, however, the thirty-eight unbound pages were given to Blake 'to dispose of for his own advantage' Blake continued to give, or perhaps sell, copies to friends and patrons until the end of his life, and there is no reason to think he ever grew ashamed of the poems' occasional crudities. It is significant that, though he corrected misprints in several copies in his own hand, he only made one attempt to improve a poem's style. (The poem in question was *Fair Elenor*, a nightmarish pseudo-ballad not included in this selection.)

Blake entered his twentieth year in November 1776, but some of the poems in *Poetical Sketches* must have been written later than this. There are obvious reminiscences of both the 'Rowley' poems (1777) and the *Miscellanies* (1778) of Thomas Chatterton, and Kitty, the black-eyed village belle who figures in three of the 'Songs', is clearly Blake's future wife Catherine Boucher (she lived at Battersea, then a village, and is known to have had dark-brown eyes), whom he did not meet until 1781. Mathew may also be responsible for the little volume's title, which is in the same apologetic strain as his 'Advertisement'. The poems written when Blake was only eleven or twelve are presumably the imitations of Spenser, Milton and Shakespeare, in which there is no trace of his later symbolism.

p. 1. TO THE MUSES

Blake's rebuke to the poets of his time is as derivative and 'literary' as anything by Collins or Joseph and Thomas Warton. And, as in the case of these poets, the main source of the poetic diction is Milton. The structural formula, on the other hand—three parallel quatrains, each with its own series of images, and a fourth quatrain summing it all up —though common in early seventeenth-century poetry (it is a natural development of the English or Shakespearian sonnet), is not to be met in Milton. Blake's immediate structural source may have been Sir Henry Wotton's 'You meaner beauties of the night'. He quotes a line from *Reliquiae Wottonianae* in *An Island in the Moon*, and Percy had also reprinted Wotton's poem in *Reliques of Ancient English Poetry*, an anthology well known to Blake (his well-thumbed copy of the first volume of the first edition is now in America).

1. *Ida's shady brow:* Blake is not likely to have known the difference between the Cretan and the Phrygian Ida. The phrase is a conflation, unconscious no doubt, of two Miltonic passages—'woody Ida's inmost grove' (*Il Penseroso*, *l*.29), and 'this drear wood,/The nodding horror of whose shady brows' (*Comus*, *ll*.37–8).

2. *the chambers of the East:* ultimately from Psalm xix. 4–5, where, however—as in *Epithalamion*, *l*.149 ('chamber of the East') and *Comus*, *l*.101 ('chamber in the East')—there is only one chamber. In Isaac Watts's *A Morning Song*, *l*.5, and James Thomson's *The Morning in the Country*, *l*.1, the noun is in the plural. Blake repeats the phrase in *To Morning* (a short invocation in blank verse also in *Poetical Sketches* but not included in this selection).

6. *green corners of the earth:* perhaps a half-memory of the Bastard's 'three corners of the world' (*King John*, v. vii. *l*.116).

11. *coral grove:* another Miltonic reminiscence ('through groves/Of coral stray' *Paradise Lost*, VII., *ll*.404–5.)

p. 1. SONG ('MY SILKS AND FINE ARRAY')

Although Blake's conscious models for both this and the next song must have been 'Come away, come away, death' (*Twelfth Night*), 'Fear no more the heat of the sun' (*Cymbeline*), and similar lyrics, his

95

third verse is clearly an echo of a stanza from the poem by Lord Vaux which Percy reprinted in the first volume of the *Reliques* from Tottel's Miscellany (1557):

> A pikeax and a spade,
>   And eke a shrowding shete,
> A house of clay for to be made
>   For such a guest most mete.

In the versified letter to Flaxman, September 12th, 1800, Blake distinguished between Milton's influence on him and Shakespeare's: 'Milton loved me in childhood and showed me his face', whereas, in contradistinction, 'Shakespeare in riper years gave me his hand'. But it is difficult to believe that more than a year or two can separate *To the Muses* and these Shakespearian songs, which have the same quality of brilliant pastiche. Perhaps in 1800 'Shakespeare' meant the plays rather than the lyrics. *Tiriel* (*c*. 1788), the first of the Prophetic Books, shows the influence of *King Lear* and *Timon of Athens*. The dramatic fragment *King Edward the Third* and the prologues for *King Edward the Fourth* and *King John*, all three included in *Poetical Sketches* and apparently written *c*. 1777, are only superficially Shakespearian, the crucial influence being Chatterton.

p. 2.   SONG ('MEMORY, HITHER COME')

2.   *And tune your merry notes:* a half-conscious reminiscence of 'And turn his merry note' (*As You Like It*, II. v. *l*.3).

8.   *the watery glass:* either from *A Midsummer Night's Dream*, I. i. *ll*.209–10 ('when Phoebe doth behold/Her silver image in the watery glass'), or possibly from Pope's *Pastorals*, ii. *l*.28 ('Fresh rising blushes paint the watery glass').

15–16.   Cp. the final lines of the interpolated song in Beaumont and Fletcher's *The Nice Valour*, 'Hence all you vain delights':

> Then stretch our bones in a still gloomy valley,
> Nothing so dainty sweet as lovely melancholy.

p. 3.   TO SPRING

Pope's *Pastorals* and Thomson's *Seasons* started a minor poetic fashion. Blake may or may not have come across John Hawkesworth's four 'odes' on the seasons, the four 'Imitations of Spenser' of Moses Mendez, the four 'Pastoral Ballads' of Thomas Brerewood, or John Scott's four seasonal 'elegies', but he must have been aware that such things were being written. Unlike Thomson's, however, the stock eighteenth-century quartet on the seasons was short and *not* in blank verse. Blake's blank verse in these poems, at once fluent and self-consciously abrupt, had almost certainly been learnt from Mark Akenside, whose *The Pleasures of the Imagination* (1744) also gave him some of his phrases. The essential difference between Blake and such poets as Akenside, Thomson and Collins is that the latter are only able to define a personified abstraction by *accumulating* epithets, images, illustrations or short disconnected incidents, whereas Blake uses the conventional attributes of the seasons as a point of departure for the *dramatic* presentation of his quasi-divine figures—Spring the angel-bridegroom, Summer the heroic embodiment of physical energy, Autumn the jovial Pan-like creature, Winter the alarming destructive giant. In these miniature dramas, as in *Mad Song* and the two *Songs* following it, Blake's mature symbolic technique is already in process of formation. In general, indeed, from this point, the interest of the imitations and borrowed phrases shifts from the boy's powers of assimilation to the new uses to which he now puts old images.

1–8. Cp. *The Pleasures of Imagination*, I., *ll*.312–17:

> Hither turn
> Thy [=beauty's] graceful footsteps; . . . let thy eyes
> Effuse the mildness of their azure dawn;
> And may the fanning breezes waft aside
> Thy radiant looks . . .

1. *with dewy locks:* cp. the description of the angel in Eve's dream, *Paradise Lost*, V., *ll*.56–7 ('his dewy locks distilled/Ambrosia').
2. *the clear windows of the morning:* a Spenserism, cp. especially *Colin Clout's Come Home Again*, *ll*.604–5:

> Her looks were like beams of the morning sun,
> Forth looking through the windows of the east.

15. *her languished head:* 'It withers on the stalk with languished head' (*Comus*, *l*.744); 'With languished head unpropped' (*Samson Agonistes*, *l*.119).

Blake was always uncomfortable in the five-stress line, and it is difficult to decide how far the weak endings of *ll.*1 (in), 4 (oft), 10 (on) and 11 (thy) are intentional. The first two stanzas only just achieve blank verse, but the discords of their long uncontrolled sentences are resolved most effectively in the end-stopped and strictly iambic third stanza.

6. *ruddy limbs and flourishing hair:* an almost exact anticipation of *l.*2 of the splendid fragment of *c.* 1792:

> Abstinence sows sand all over
> The ruddy limbs and flaming hair,
> But Desire gratified
> Plants fruits of life and beauty there.

14. *silver wire:* 'All sounds on fret by string or golden wire' (*Paradise Lost,* vii. *l.*597).

The abrupt conclusion suggests Akenside's influence again, and his account of 'laughing Autumn' (*The Pleasures of the Imagination,* I., *ll.*288 ff.) may have provided Blake's point of departure.

10. *modest Eve:* cp. Collins's *Ode to Evening* (Dodsley version), *ll.*1, 2:

> If aught of oaten stop, or pastoral song,
> May hope, chaste Eve, to soothe thy modest ear . . .

1. A more obviously symbolic development of this image is to be found in *The Book of Thel* (1789), *l.*108:

> The eternal gates' terrific porter lifted the northern bar.

9–10. Cp. the description of the 'monster' (Danger) in Collins's *Ode to Fear* (1747):

> whose limbs of giant mould
> What mortal eye can fixed behold?
> Who stalks his round, an hideous form,
> Howling amidst the midnight storm,
> Or throws him on the ridgy steep
> Of some loose hanging rock to sleep.

Blake has concentrated Collins's diffuse rhetoric into two remarkably vivid lines.

15–16. Perhaps partly suggested by *The Pleasures of Imagination*, II., *ll.*9–10 ('the gloomy north, with iron swarms/Tempestuous pouring from her frozen caves').

p. 6. MAD SONG

Percy's *Reliques of Ancient English Poetry* has no less than six separate 'Mad Songs', all of them characterized by more or less metrical variety and logical irrelevance. The one closest to Blake's is perhaps *The Distracted Lover* of Henry Carey, the author of *Sally in our Alley*, who had committed suicide as recently as 1743.

2. *a-cold:* already an archaism in Blake's time. An allusion is presumably intended to Edgar's 'Tom's a-cold' (*King Lear*, III. iv. *l.*59).

7. *rustling birds:* 'beds' in *Poetical Sketches*, but the misprint is corrected to 'birds' in at least four of the surviving copies in Blake's own hand. Blake repeats the phrase at the beginning of *The Couch of Death*, the first of three prose-poems at the end of *Poetical Sketches*. It was a favourite of James Macpherson's in his Ossianic forgeries (which Blake, with many of his contemporaries, always accepted as genuine).

p. 7. SONG ('HOW SWEET I ROAMED')

A foretaste of Blake's later symbolic method. Verses iii. and iv. extend and clinch through the parallel symbols the argument initiated and defined in i. and ii. The boy who has allowed himself to be lured into the Prince of Love's garden must be considered identical, for the purposes of the poem, with the song-bird the same god has trapped and is mocking in its golden cage. And the moral is the same for boy and bird—a distrust of apparent kindness and flattery that disguise, under the aesthetic titillations they provide, the actual 'loss of liberty'. According to B. H. Malkin (*A Father's Memoirs of his Child*, 1806), who must have got the information from Blake himself, the poem 'was written before the age of fourteen'. In that case the biographical reality underlying the symbolism may be the proposal his father is known to have made to apprentice Blake to a fashionable painter. He *was* fourteen when, this scheme having been dropped, he was finally apprenticed to the engraver Basire. There are suggestive similarities in the imagery to *The Schoolboy* (p. 47 above) in *Songs of Experience* that seem to confirm some such an interpretation.

3. *the Prince of Love:* the mythological figure Luvah is sometimes called 'The prince of Love' in *The Four Zoas* (Nights i, ix.), but the term is not in general use in Blake's later writings. On the other hand, both Christ and Cupid seem inappropriate in the poem's general context. 10. *Phoebus fired my vocal rage:* the god of poetry inspired me.

Extracts from AN ISLAND IN THE MOON

The manuscript of this entertaining fragment, minus a leaf or two, is now in the Fitzwilliam Museum, Cambridge. Blake's intentions in writing as much as he did are unknown and not easy to guess. There is no title—the name under which it usually passes is an editorial concoction based on the first sentence ('In the Moon is a certain Island . . .')—and the end is so abrupt that it is clearly not an end at all. On internal evidence it is now dated *c.* December 1784, and much industry and ingenuity have been spent in attempted identifications of the *dramatis personae*.

Some interesting and persuasive suggestions by D. V. Erdman will be found in his *Blake: Prophet Against Empire* (Princeton, 1954). But except that Quid the Cynic may very well be Blake himself and that Inflammable Gas the Windfinder is the eminent chemist-theologian Joseph Priestley, little agreement has been reached so far as to who they all are. Not that it matters much. The personal satire, in so far as there was any, is secondary to the general spirit of 'nonsense', anticipating Lewis Carroll in the prose and Edward Lear in some of the songs, that pervades these extraordinary conversations. At the conversaziones dispensed by the Mathews and via the acquaintances Blake was making through his artist friends, like Flaxman and Thomas Stothard, and Joseph Johnson, the genial and hospitable publisher, Blake had begun at this time to get to know some of London's antiquarian cranks, eccentric philosophers, amateur philologists and would-be blue-stockings and ladies of fashion. And *An Island in the Moon* is his high-spirited comment on it all. That is about all it seems necessary to say. The Innocence of which he was about to make himself the prophet was not, it is clear, the innocence of ignorance.

SONGS OF INNOCENCE AND OF EXPERIENCE

Songs of Innocence was the first of the poetical works to be published by the special process of relief-etching on copper followed by hand-tinting in water-colours that Blake called 'Illuminated Printing'. The illustrated title-page is dated 1789, but as it was his regular practice in his later works to begin the engraving with the title-page, 1789 is not necessarily the year in which the thirty-one plates of illustrated or decorated text that make up *Songs of Innocence* in its final form were completed. Until he had acquired fluency from practice the necessity, as in all engraving of the written word, to cut a *mirror-image* of the text of each poem must have made every plate a formidably laborious undertaking. (The first experiment in Illuminated Printing, the prose tractate *There is No Natural Religion*, which immediately preceded *Songs of Innocence*, went wrong because Blake engraved the imprint on the title-page 'The Author and Printer W. Blake' in *reversed* characters.) In any case no copies of *Songs of Innocence* have survived that we can be certain were issued in 1789. The fact is more than a bibliographical nicety, because it provides additional evidence of the continuity of Blake's lyrical development from *Poetical Sketches* to *Songs of Experience*. What it means is that, though no doubt most of the Songs of Innocence had been written by 1789, a few *may* be later—just as a few others are certainly much earlier. Four of the songs were undoubtedly in existence in 1784. One is the early version of *Laughing Song*, which was copied out by an unidentified admirer with two similar 'Songs by Mr. Blake' on to the flyleaf of a copy of *Poetical Sketches* that bears the inscription 'from Mrs. Flaxman May 15 1784'. And among the heterogeneous songs that are sung in *An Island in the Moon*, which was written towards the end of 1784, are earlier versions of *Nurse's Song, Holy Thursday* and *The Little Boy Lost*. The fact that at least five years, and possibly six or even seven years, divides the composition of these poems from their illustration in *Songs of Innocence* suggests another critical corollary. It is simply that too much confidence must not be placed in the illustrations as providing clues to the interpretation of the symbolism. The Blake who engraved the poems was an altogether different man, with a totally different outlook on life, from the young man who wrote them. And a similar caveat applies, or may apply, with various degrees of probability, to many of the other Songs of Innocence as well as to almost all the Songs of Experience (see page 104 below). The illustration of *The Blossom*, for example, has been used to give that poem an elaborate phallic interpretation—which has been widely accepted—that would never occur to anyone who had only the words in front of him. And in the case of the first plate of *The Little Girl Lost*, with its mature pair of lovers instead of the solitary seven-year-old Lyca of the text, it almost looks as if Blake had forgotten which song he was illustrating. (If the lovers are Lyca's parents they have no business on that plate.) It is wiser generally to look for the meaning of obscure lines not in the engravings but in the songs' words.

The Songs of Innocence can be divided into three strata, corresponding to the three periods in Blake's life in which they seem to have been written. The 1784 songs are all addressed to adults and not to children. They are closely connected with the later songs in *Poetical Sketches*, and like them they can reasonably be seen as a reflection of the ecstatic happiness of the years following Blake's marriage. In terms of literary history they represent a culmination of the cult of poetic 'simplicity' that began with Addison and his associates—Ambrose Philips, Thomas Tickell, Henry Carey, etc.—and that, running through Shenstone, Collins and Percy to the so-called 'Della Cruscans', prepared the way for *Lyrical Ballads*. Their Innocence is essentially a pastoral innocence, more sentimental than Christian, and with overtones of the classical Golden Age rather than of the Garden of Eden.

A second stratum is made up of the poems specifically addressed to children, such as *The Lamb, The Shepherd, The Little Black Boy* and *The Blossom*. These *are* Christian poems, and they are often consciously didactic ('So if all do their duty they need not fear harm'). They belong to another recognized eighteenth-century genre, that of Bunyan's *Book for Boys and Girls* (1686), Isaac Watts's *Divine Songs Attempted in Easy Language for the Use of Children* (1715), a book that Blake knew well under its later title *Divine and Moral Songs*, and their numerous imitations (principally by Nonconformists) down to the *Hymns in Prose for Children* (1781) of Mrs. Barbauld, a nice Unitarian schoolmistress and poetess that Blake must almost certainly have met at Joseph Johnson's. An important difference is that Blake wrote most of these Christian-didactic pieces, which make up some two-thirds of the original *Songs of Innocence*, with at least one eye on their future illustration by himself. The collection is first of all a children's picture-book. The engraved title-page, with its illustration of an extremely straight-backed elderly female who is showing a large picture-book to a fascinated little boy and girl, puts it firmly in its contemporary context. Between the autumn of 1784 and the first half of 1787 Blake and James Parker kept a print-shop next door to the family hosiery in Broad Street, and a collection of moral songs for children with coloured pictures in it would obviously have made an attractive and appropriate addition to

Blake and Parker's meagre stock. But if the songs were written at this time, as many of them probably were, Blake did not hit on the medium for their illustration until a year or two later. According to J. T. Smith, who had been a personal friend of Robert Blake's, the process of Illuminated Printing was only expounded to William by Robert's ghost in a vision *after* his death. The story rings true. At any rate Robert did die in February 1787, and according to the colophon of *The Ghost of Abel* (1822), the last of the engraved poems (it is an unhappy post-script to Byron's *Cain*), 'Blake's Original Stereotype was 1788'.

The third stratum in *Songs of Innocence* includes four poems—*The Little Girl Lost, The Little Girl Found, The Schoolboy,* and *The Voice of the Ancient Bard*—that were finally transferred to *Songs of Experience.* The characteristic tone of these poems, and of one or two others like them, is more sombre and more adult than either of the other groups. Their author has abandoned the rôle he claims in the *Introduction* ('Piping down the valleys wild') of the happy carefree piper for that of a prophet ('In futurity/I prophetic see') and inspired 'bard'. Even the questions his reluctant schoolboy asks society represent a significant change in attitude as well as in rhetorical form. (The earlier Songs make statements instead of asking questions; when a question *is* asked, as in *The Lamb* or *Infant Joy*, it is answered immediately.) *A Dream* also appears as a Song of Experience in some early copies of the combined series, though Blake soon restored it to Innocence. No doubt it is less out of place there, but it resembles *The Little Girl Lost* and *The Little Girl Found* in having an unhappy beginning and middle and a happy mystical end. *Night*, the greatest of the Songs of Innocence, also has obvious parallels with *The Little Girl Lost* and *The Little Girl Found*, although unlike them it was never transferred to Experience. *The Voice of the Ancient Bard* has the words of its text engraved in italic lettering, whereas all the other Songs are in minuscule roman—a technical difference that suggests it may have been engraved some time after them. In most copies it comes at the very end of *Songs of Innocence*. A more interesting difference is that in its message it has left behind the worlds of the pastoral and the nursery for contemporary social and political realities. Its 'truth new-born' may be Swedenborgianism or the French Revolution, or perhaps a combina-tion of both of them, but whatever the precise meaning may be some-thing new is clearly being attempted, even if it does not quite come off. This stratum can perhaps be dated *c.* 1788–90. The new interests and tone parallel Blake's gradual transition to a tragic philosophy of life in

Tiriel (c. 1788), *The Book of Thel* (engraved 1789), and the marginalia in his copies of Lavater (early 1789) and Swedenborg (1789–90). In any case his uncertainty whether to ascribe these poems to Innocence or Experience differentiates them sharply from the songs that the piper promised 'Every child may joy to hear'. It is not 'joy' that characterizes *Night* or *The Little Girl Lost* and *The Little Girl Found*, but a mystical certainty beyond either happiness or unhappiness.

The certainty proved more precarious than Blake had anticipated— as *Songs of Experience* is there to prove. In October 1793 he issued a characteristic 'Prospectus' or sale catalogue of his engravings with the prices at which they could be bought. It included 'Songs of Innocence, in Illuminated Printing' and 'Songs of Experience in Illuminated Printing', each being obtainable for five shillings. The announcement certainly suggests (i) that *Songs of Experience* had been engraved by 1793, and (ii) that copies of it could be purchased separately. All the surviving copies, however, have the date 1794 on the title-page and show no sign whatever of having been issued separately. The whole point of *Songs of Experience* being the detailed contrast and deflation it presents to *Songs of Innocence*, the two series *have* to be read together. By way of underlining this interrelationship, Blake added in or about 1794 a fine general title-page for both series which reads 'Songs of Innocence and Of Experience Shewing the Two Contrary States of the Human Soul'. The plate, an illustration of Experience rather than Innocence, shows a young Adam and Eve, naked except for their fig-leaves (which look more like vine-leaves), cowering in agonized terror before the leaping flames of God's anger. (It is reproduced as the frontispiece to this selection.)

Some four or five years, then, separate the engraving of *Songs of Innocence*, or most of the plates at any rate, from *Songs of Experience*. There is no similar gap between the composition of the last Songs of Innocence and the first Songs of Experience. Indeed, as we have seen, Blake eventually discovered that four of the later Songs of Innocence were sufficiently close to being Songs of Experience to merit inclusion in that series. Some of these transitional songs may have been written as late as 1790, and as the earliest of the Songs of Experience proper seem to have been written in 1791, they are a more reliable guide to the latter's meaning than the much later engravings. The position is much the same as with *Songs of Innocence*. The illustrations and decorations are attractive and occasionally impressive—for example, the moving and beautiful *Holy Thursday* (Experience)—*in themselves*, but as a commentary on points of detail in the meaning of the poems they are normally unhelpful if not actually misleading. In some of the engraved copies, for instance, the rose of *The Sick Rose* is not red but white—whereas the whole point of the poem is the suggestion of naked flesh in the rose's colour.

Incomparably the best commentary on *Songs of Experience* is the notebook now generally known as the Rossetti MS.[1] The Rossetti MS. is an extraordinary document. Almost every inch of its 116 pages is covered with poems and doggerel, in every state of completion and incompletion, all sorts and varieties of prose, and dozens of more or less elaborate sketches in various media. Its total effect on the reader of Blake is like that of Keats's letters on the reader of Keats. It adds a new dimension to one's understanding. Originally it had been a sketchbook. Five of the early pages have drawings and sketches in a curiously stiff and angular style, quite unlike Blake's fluent curves, that have been attributed to his brother Robert (who died of consumption in 1787). When Blake acquired the notebook he began by using it sideways for sketches. (They start at the other end of the notebook from Robert's, only every other page being used so that the drawing can overflow on to the page below, and they continue up to page 96.) As far as they are decipherable these sketches appear to be illustrations of scenes in or suggested by *Paradise Lost*, and they can no doubt be connected with Joseph Johnson's abortive scheme for a magnificent illustrated Milton by Henry Fuseli that Blake was to engrave and Cowper the poet to edit.[2] The drawings, especially the nudes, have the new vigour of line that Blake was now learning from Fuseli, and they may perhaps be dated 1790-1. About this time, or a few months later, Blake began to

[1] Dante Gabriel Rossetti 'discovered' it and owned it for years. Rossetti bought it in 1847, for ten shillings, from William Palmer—a brother of Samuel Palmer the painter, one of Blake's most ardent disciples—who had somehow acquired it from Blake's widow. The MS. is now in the British Museum; an excellent facsimile edited by Geoffrey Keynes was published by the Nonesuch Press in 1935. Photographs of the pages on which first drafts of the Songs of Experience (and the associated poems) appear are also to be found in Joseph H. Wicksteed's *Blake's Innocence and Experience* (1928), where the reproduction is decidedly clearer than in the Nonesuch edition.

[2] See John Knowles, *Life and Writings of Henry Fuseli* (1831), i., 172. On discovering in 1792 that John Boydell, a rival publisher who had recently issued a successful illustrated Shakespeare, was also planning an illustrated Milton, Johnson decided to limit the project to the unillustrated edition by Cowper that was published after the latter's death by Hayley.

use the same end of the notebook for the poems that are the nucleus of *Songs of Experience*. Instead of using the pages sideways he now turned the notebook upside down and, starting with its last page but one (page 115), worked his way steadily back to page 98. The pages opposite the *Paradise Lost* drawings had generally been left blank, and when the sketch only consisted of a few tentative lines Blake did not hesitate to overwrite it with poems. Normally, however, the even-numbered pages have a *Paradise Lost* drawing sideways on the page ('Satan exulting over Eve', 'Satan defying God the Father, the Son interceding', 'The Trinity', 'Adam and Eve', etc.), while the odd-numbered pages, generally divided into two columns, contain the poems. Sometimes the poem's text is left without corrections, but most of the poems show deletions, alterations or additions, the revisions of *Earth's Answer* and *The Tiger* actually spilling over on to the illustrations.

It has been necessary to describe the Rossetti MS. with this degree of minuteness, because the physical conditions under which the Songs of Experience were written probably contributed to their meaning. These poems are not fair copies. In the Rossetti MS. we see Blake in the actual process of composition, and the poems obviously follow one another, with one or two possible exceptions, in the order in which they were written. May not the cramped conditions under which Blake was writing have unconsciously encouraged a greater verbal concentration than he usually achieved? The question is at least worth asking. Moreover the notebook probably once belonged to Robert, and as such it would always possess a special sanctity for Blake. 'Thirteen years ago', he wrote to Hayley in May 1800, 'I lost a brother, and with his spirit I converse daily and hourly in the spirit, and see him in my remembrance, in the regions of my imagination. I hear his advice, and even now write from his dictate.' Under these circumstances Blake may well have derived a special psychological stimulus from the notebook as an aid in the act of composition, a stimulus that would more than counterbalance the physical inconveniences that it created. The fact that he in time filled almost every blank inch in it certainly suggests that it did finally acquire for Blake some special spiritual virtue of its own. Nothing less, for instance, will explain the haphazard and untidy way in which Blake's last important poem, *The Everlasting Gospel*, is scattered through empty corners of the notebook. When the Songs of Experience were being written there were still, of course, plenty of blank pages left, but the compulsion not to waste the precious paper may have already begun to operate. If it did, the tendency to concision, an almost epigrammatic brevity, that characterizes all the poems, early and late, in the Rossetti MS. would follow naturally. (The contrast with the general diffuseness, not only of the Prophetic Books, but of many of the earlier poems, too, certainly invites some such an explanation.)

Blake cannot have been unaware, either, of the sketches for *Paradise Lost*. As he looked up from the first verse of *Earth's Answer* the contorted figure of Satan shrieking his defiance of God the Father would have met his eyes. And even when there could be no specific influence the drawings would at least tend to confirm and reinforce the background of Genesis myth in the poems. The symbolism of Experience draws heavily on the Fall of Man, the Fall of the Angels, the forbidden fruit, the serpent-tempter, and similar themes. The fact that Blake had recently been illustrating Genesis episodes and that the illustrations were often before his eyes as he worked out what were often their poetic equivalents is one that needs to be remembered in reading them.

There are sixty-one poems or poetical fragments in the last twenty pages of the Rossetti MS. How long a period their composition occupied it is difficult to determine, but my impression—partly derived from the handwriting, which varies noticeably both in the size of letters and the degree of its slope after page 105, and partly from the poems themselves —is that the first twenty or thirty pieces were written close together and that the others were spread over a much longer interval. Unfortunately the only poem in the Experience group that can be dated at all precisely is the last of the series. This describes in ballad form Lafayette's final betrayal, as it seemed to Blake, of the cause of the Revolution and the ironical reward of immediate imprisonment meted out to him by the Austrians when he crossed their border in August 1792. The news of Lafayette's fate did not reach England until the end of October, and Blake's poem would still have been topical in November or December 1792, though hardly later. This is a solid *terminus ad quem*. The *terminus a quo*, or the date when the poems began, is perhaps suggested by the twelfth poem in the series ('Why should I care for the men of Thames'), which contains two couplets that may be topical:—

(i)   the little blasts of fear
       That the hireling blows into my ear . . .
(ii) The Ohio shall wash his stains from me,
       I was born a slave but I go to be free.

The two allusions cannot be said to *prove* anything, but they combine to suggest that the poem was written in 1791, or perhaps early 1792. The 'little blasts of fear' may well refer to the circumstances under which Blake's poem *The French Revolution* was suppressed. Joseph Johnson printed this curious poem, or rather the first of its seven books, in 1791, but for some reason it was never actually published. Now, as it happens, Johnson had also printed and then failed to publish the first volume of Tom Paine's *Rights of Man* in the February of the same year. No doubt he was afraid of a Government prosecution in both cases. It is true that Paine did find another publisher, but within the year booksellers were being gaoled for selling it. Paine's revolutionary enthusiams may also be responsible for the new glamour the Ohio had now acquired for Blake. Paine and Joel Barlow, a minor American poet whom Blake had read, were Joseph Johnson's guests from time to time from the spring of 1791 to the autumn of 1792, and Blake undoubtedly saw something of both of them. The indications are a bit nebulous, but they suggest to me a date in or about the summer or autumn of 1791.

If the poems of Experience in the Rossetti MS. can be dated 1791–2 only a few months will have separated the last of the Songs of Innocence from the earliest of the Songs of Experience. The probability is of great interest because it provides one more example of the continuity of Blake's poetry. It is clear that Mary Wollstonecraft's advances, if she was indeed the disturbing influence, and the repercussions set up in Blake by his wife's jealousy, were only the climax to a process of gradual disillusionment that can be traced back to *Tiriel* and the prose tractates on natural religion, both of which are generally dated 1788, which may have had its emotional origins for Blake in Robert's death in 1787. *The Marriage of Heaven and Hell*, which was certainly started in 1790, reflects a similar disillusionment with Swedenborgianism. And the mood persisted after the Experience group in the Rossetti MS. came to an end in *Fayette*, as is shown by the four poems in *Songs of Experience* in its final form that are neither in the Rossetti MS. nor in the early copies of *Songs of Innocence*. The four are the *Introduction* ('Hear the voice of the Bard'), *A Little Girl Lost*, *Ah! Sunflower* and *To Tirzah*, and they were presumably all written after the pieces in the Rossetti MS. About *To Tirzah*, indeed, there can be no question. Tirzah, the materialistic antithesis to Jerusalem, is a figure that was only added at a late stage in the evolution of Blake's mythological system. The early copies of *Songs of Experience* do not contain the poem at all, and it was probably written about 1800. The three other poems, all of them incomparably superior to *To Tirzah*, were presumably composed in 1793.

The preceding analysis has been primarily concerned to establish the order in which the Songs of Innocence and Experience were written. A chronological framework is the indispensable preliminary to the understanding of Blake's poetry. Unlike the poetry of Pope, for example, or that of Mr. T. S. Eliot, Blake's progress was not through a succession of distinct styles, with intervals in which little or nothing is written. On the contrary, the controlling principle is one of continuous growth, an almost organic development of the symbolism, the poetic structure and the underlying human situations demanding communication. With one exception the poems are printed here in the order of their composition, so far as that is determinable. The exception is the group of poems that show 'the Two Contrary States of the Human Soul' in a detailed dramatic opposition between Innocence and Experience. Here, instead of following Blake's own haphazard arrangement of the plates (an order that varies almost from copy to copy and in which no intelligible method has ever been recognized in the chaos), it has seemed better to follow the spirit of Blake's intentions by printing the Song of Innocence first, with as far as possible the Experience counterpart facing it on the right-hand page. As the order in which the various Songs of Experience were composed is known, the knowledge has been allowed to determine the sequence of 'contraries'. Nor is this order simply a matter of editorial convenience. The fact that Blake felt himself impelled to write a disillusioning version of *A Cradle Song* and *Infant Joy* some time before meting out similar treatments to *The Chimney Sweeper* and *Holy Thursday* has obvious and interesting implications. Although there has been this drastic interference with Blake's arrangement of the poems—an interference, however, that Blake himself could hardly have failed to commend in a modern edition that does not reproduce the original illustrations—there are no omissions here from *Songs of Innocence and of Experience*. Reluctantly, however, the associated pieces in the Rossetti MS. have been reduced to a bare selection. But there is only one sensible way to read the lesser items in the Rossetti MS. and that is in the facsimile.[1]

---

[1] A short summary of the contents of the Rossetti MS. may be useful. Blake used the notebook off and on for some twenty years, and it is possible to distinguish seven separate layers in the entries and sketches:

(i) The sketches by Robert Blake. (It is just possible they are not by Robert *p.* 15. GENERAL TITLE. *Songs of Innocence and of Experience:* the word 'innocence' turns up in most neo-classic discussions of pastoral poetry; it had much the same primitivistic connotation as 'simplicity', an even more popular critical *cliché.* Blake uses either the noun or the adjective several times in the later songs in *Poetical Sketches* and in their immediate successors the MS. *Song by a Shepherd* and *Song by an Old Shepherd* (not included in this selection). In *Songs of Innocence* itself the only instances are 'the lamb's innocent call' in *The Shepherd* and the 'innocent faces' and 'innocent hands' of *Holy Thursday* (both are also in the version in *An Island in the Moon*). The noun 'experience' turns up in its usual sense in *King Edward the Third* and the verb in its philosophical sense in the prose tractate *All Religions are One* (1788), but it is clear the word then had none of the symbolic overtones for Blake that 'innocence' had acquired *c.* 1783–4. The first occasion on which Blake specifically opposes the two words is in *Motto to the Songs of Innocence and of Experience*, a poem that comes towards the end of the Experience group in the Rossetti MS. and can therefore be dated 1792. In this poem Experience

---

but e.g. by Kate Blake, William's wife, who had some talent too.) (Pp. 5, 7, 9, 11, 13.) Before 1787?

(ii) Blake's sketches for the projected illustrated edition of *Paradise Lost.* (Sideways, starting from the end of the notebook, pp. 112, 110–11, 108, 106, 104, 102, 100, 98, 96.) 1790–1?

(iii) The Experience group of poems. (Upside down, starting from the end of the notebook, pp. 115, 114, 113, 111, 109, 108, 107, 106, 105, 103, 101, 100, 99, 98.) 1791–2?

(iv) Some fifty or sixty sketches for *The Gates of Paradise* (published by Blake May 17th, 1793). Only twenty of the sketches were finally engraved, but the figures by the side both of these sketches and other similarly emblematic drawings include a '68', and Blake probably contemplated a much larger volume when making them. (Normally a vignette in the centre of what at the time was a blank page, beginning p. 15, sometimes on alternate pages and sometimes consecutively, up to p. 97.) 1792–3?

(v) Some five sketches for *Visions of the Daughters of Albion* (engraved title-page dated 1793), and several others subsequently utilized in *The Marriage of Heaven and Hell, Songs of Experience* and *Europe* (all engraved 1793–4), though apparently not made specifically as illustrations to these works. (Scattered haphazardly in the blanks left after the sketches for *The Gates of Paradise* had been completed; some may be contemporary with them.) 1793?

(vi) Sketches for Hayley's *Ballads,* first drafts of a few lyrics, epigrams and oddments—all dating from the end of the Felpham period. 1803?

(vii) Drafts of the *Public Address* and *Vision of the Last Judgment* (both in prose); *The Eternal Gospel*; epigrams, gnomic verses, personal jottings (in prose), etc. 1808–11?

is not much more than the self-protective caution that 'the Good' need to acquire in a world of knaves and hypocrites. By the time Blake was writing *The Four Zoas*, Night ii., Experience has a more positive content:

> What is the price of Experience? do men buy it for a song?
> Or wisdom for a dance in the street? No, it is bought with the price
> Of all that a man hath, his houses, his wife, his children.

Experience is almost identical here with wisdom. A later note written on the back of *The Four Zoas*, Night vii., indicates Blake's final position: 'Unorganized Innocence: an impossibility. Innocence dwells with Wisdom, but never with Ignorance.'

p. 15. INTRODUCTION (INNOCENCE)

Who is the child on the cloud? In so far as *Songs of Innocence* is a collection of moral songs for children the child must be, in some sense, the infant Jesus. Blake's capital in the word 'Lamb' (*l.*5) seems to confirm this interpretation. Moreover, although clouds are usually an oppression-symbol in Blake, the Bible authorizes their use as the chariot of divinity. But the poem is also full of the conventional properties of pastoral poetry—a piper who is also a singer, wild nature, reeds, running water, etc., as well as the device of formal dialogue—and all this adds up to suggest nothing much more supernatural than the Spirit of Poetry. The presence of three separate distinguishable strata in *Songs of Innocence* (see p. 104 above) would tend no doubt to discourage Blake from defining too closely their common source of inspiration.

8. *he wept to hear:* cp. the Proverb of Hell (p. 67 above), 'Excess of sorrow laughs. Excess of joy weeps.'

18. *I stained the water clear:* either to make his ink or to prepare the water-colours for tinting the engravings. *The Little Girl Lost*, *l.*4, 'Grave the sentence deep', also specifies the medium Blake was employing to write his songs 'In a book, that all may read'.

p. 16. INTRODUCTION (EXPERIENCE)

A difficult poem that needs to be read with its sequel *Earth's Answer*, if it is not to be misunderstood. (Although the order of the other songs varies from copy to copy, *Earth's Answer* follows the *Introduction* in every extant copy of *Songs of Experience*.) Blake's problem was to summarize dramatically (in dialogue) the essential themes of the Songs of Experience in the way in which 'Piping down the valleys wild' had so successfully introduced the reader to what he would find in *Songs of Innocence*. But as the essential message of Songs of Experience was the inadequacy of Innocence in eighteenth-century England the poem had also to be as different as possible from its predecessor. Instead of the merry Piper, an all-wise Bard; instead of prelapsarian content, the agonies of conflict and oppression after the Fall; instead of a benevolent Christ-Muse, a divine tyrant (Jehovah) and a tyrannized Earth; instead of day, night; instead of poetic lucidity, prophetic obscurity; instead of one poem, two connected poems that would exemplify in their oppositions the Doctrine of Contraries which provided the metaphysical justification of the Two Contrary States.

Some of the difficulties undoubtedly derive from Blake's decision to use *Earth's Answer* in this scheme. Unlike 'Hear the voice of the Bard' it was not a poem written especially for the occasion. It was already some eighteen months old at the time the former was written, and the question it had originally provided Earth's answer to was not quite the same question. In the Rossetti MS. (which does not include 'Hear the voice of the Bard') *Earth's Answer* comes immediately after the following fragment:

> Thou hast a lap full of seed,
> And this is a fine country.
> Why dost thou not cast thy seed,
> And live in it merrily?
>
> Shall I cast it on the sand
> And turn it into fruitful land?
> For on no other ground
> Can I sow my seed,
> Without tearing up
> Some stinking weed.

In their context in the Rossetti MS. it is clear that these lines are the masculine answer to the problem of what Blake called 'free love', by which he meant the ideal sexual relationship. The only alternatives are marriage with all its restrictions on the individual's liberty ('sand') and adultery or fornication ('some stinking weed'). *Earth's Answer* put the feminine point of view. Women are bound in the same bondage of conventional sexual morality as men, and they too would welcome a return to the sincerity and frankness without which love cannot fulfil its great creative function. The images of man as the farmer and woman as the potentially fertile soil are complementary symbols. But in 'Hear the voice of the Bard' Earth is not woman but 'the lapsed soul', i.e. Adam (or perhaps Adam and Eve), and 'the break of day' is not a sexual millennium but a political or religious one. And so the appeal 'O Earth, O Earth, return!', which is clearly addressed to mankind in general, really requires a different answer from the one it gets. A general issue is reduced to a particular one.

There are also some lesser difficulties, mainly due to the ambiguity of Blake's pronouns. It is the Holy Word (Jehovah, the God of the Old Testament) who calls 'the lapsed soul' (*l.*6) and weeps (*l.*7), not the Bard. (The 'Calling' and 'weeping' are what the Bard's 'ears have heard'.) *Ll.*11–20, as *Earth's Answer* demonstrates, are spoken by the Holy Word. 'Earth' (*l.*11) can be equated with 'the lapsed soul' (*l.*6), 'the dewy grass referring back to 'the evening dew', and 'fallen, fallen light' is probably Lucifer. (The poem is essentially *Paradise Lost* re-told to suit eighteenth-century realities.)

A possible paraphrase might be: Attend carefully, O reader, to the poems of this prophet-seer, who heard Jehovah calling Adam in the Garden of Eden after the Fall. If He wished to, Jehovah could restore Satan to Heaven, but instead He appeals pathetically (hypocritically?) to mankind to return to His worship, assuring us that the dawn of a new era is about to break and that we will not have to put up with oppression and materialism much longer.

3–7. 'And they heard the voice of the Lord God walking in the garden in the cool of the day: and Adam and his wife hid themselves from the presence of the Lord God amongst the trees of the garden' (*Genesis* iii. 8). A cancelled reading in *Earth's Answer, l.*12, makes it certain that it is the Holy Word that weeps and not the lapsed soul.

4.   *The Holy Word:* the negative morality of the Decalogue. Cp. *A Little Girl Lost,* ll.27–9:

> But his loving look,
> Like the Holy Book,
> All her tender limbs with terror shook.

5.   *the ancient trees:* a forest is one of Blake's regular oppression-symbols.
9.   *The starry pole:* the firmament or sky; it is starry (an oppression-symbol) because Jehovah prefers night to day.

10. *And fallen, fallen light renew:* 'How art thou fallen from heaven. O Lucifer, son of the morning' (*Isaiah* xiv. 12).

11. *O Earth, O Earth:* Earth is depicted, with the three other elements, in *The Gates of Paradise*, the emblematic picture-book that Blake published about the time this poem was being written (1793). A primitive and enormously muscular nude, he is painfully emerging from a 'slumberous mass'. A preliminary sketch for the plate in the Rossetti MS. has the epigraph, 'Rest rest, perturbed spirit. Shakespeare'. 18-19: 'watery shore' (*Faerie Queene*, III. vi. 45); 'watery floor' (*Lycidas*, 167). These are also oppression-symbols. The sea (the opposite of land) is cold, alarming, destructive (like night, the opposite of day); the sea-coast is land's end, a limiting principle, which separates one nation from another; a sea-cave is a symbolic prison.

20. *till the break of day:* 'till' seems to mean 'only until' as in *America*, *l.*217 ('Till Angels and weak men twelve years should govern o'er the strong'). The day that is about to break is presumably the new era initiated by the American and French Revolutions. Thus in *America* (engraved 1793), *l.*60, Orc, the Spirit of Revolution, announces that 'shadows pass, the morning 'gins to break'. *The Voice of the Ancient Bard* (written *c.* 1790), a poem that Blake seems to be half-remembering in *Introduction*, begins with a similar vague reference to the revolutionary dawn (see p. 48 above).

p. 17. EARTH'S ANSWER

3. *Her light fled:* Blake's first attempt at the line in the Rossetti MS., 'Her eyes fled', makes the intended meaning clear.

10. *the Father of the Ancient Men:* the Holy Word of the *Introduction*. In the Rossetti MS. the poem immediately following *Earth's Answer* is *In a Myrtle Shade* (see p. 55 above). There, however, the 'Father' who forbids free love is killed by the enraged lover (i.e. Blake turns atheist?) —a logical conclusion to the agonized bitterness of *Earth's Answer*. But in the less personal and more detached context of the *Introduction* it is essential for the reader to accord a measure of awe and sympathy to Jehovah. The essence of the Doctrine of Contraries was that neither pole was ultimately more 'right' than the other. Unfortunately the balance of opposites that is successfully communicated by the *Introduction* is contradicted by every line of *Earth's Answer*, in which nothing whatever is conceded to Jehovah.

11-15. This stanza was cancelled in the Rossetti MS. version, no doubt when Blake realized that the original rhyme-scheme had broken down. Ll.16–20 were then written to take its place, but though that was an improvement as far as the rhyming was concerned—*l*.16 originally read, 'Does spring hide its delight' to rhyme with 'night'—the full scheme was not achieved there either. When engraving the poem Blake rightly decided to include both stanzas in spite of the imperfections of rhyme. The rough technical edges of *Earth's Answer*, a guarantee of its burning sincerity, are an essential part of its meaning.

p. 18. A CRADLE SONG (INNOCENCE)

No doubt suggested by the attractive *A Cradle Hymn*, which is in a similar metre, at the end of Isaac Watts's *Divine and Moral Songs*—a book that Blake knew very well indeed.

4. *By happy, silent, moony beams:* 'with' or perhaps 'and' is clearly what Blake meant.

12, 16, 32. *beguiles:* a favourite word of Blake's at this period meaning 'charms away' (Innocence), 'tricks, deceives' (Experience).

p. 19. A CRADLE SONG (EXPERIENCE)

Although clearly written as a 'contrary' to the Innocence *Cradle Song*, Blake did not engrave this poem. It was his first full-scale attempt to parody or complement realistically a Song of Innocence, and he may not have been satisfied with it. The title, which has been squeezed in at the top of the page in small letters in the Rossetti MS., seems to have been an afterthought. No doubt the project of a second series of songs that would include disillusioned versions of most of the Songs of Innocence—a project that required the use as far as possible of the *same* titles—took some time to formulate itself in Blake's mind. The *Motto to the Songs of Innocence and of Experience*, which is the earliest conclusive evidence of its complete formulation, comes towards the end of the Experience group of poems in the Rossetti MS.

p. 20. INFANT JOY

5. Although abstract nouns were a staple source of Christian names in the eighteenth century, girls were not often, in fact, called Joy then.

p. 20. INFANT SORROW

In the Rossetti MS. these are the first two verses of a poem that runs to nine verses altogether which has only used the contrast with *Infant Joy* as a point of departure for a symbolic denunciation of the corrupting influence of the conventional Christian attitude to marriage. Clearly Blake had not yet reached the formula of 'contrary states', which would not have permitted the formlessness that resulted from the use of a Song of Innocence simply as an irrelevant stimulus. The salvaging of the two brilliant opening verses is a nice example of the acute technical self-criticism that Blake possessed at this time.

4. *Like a fiend hid in a cloud:* Blake had already used this line in the early *Mad Song* of *Poetical Sketches* ('Like a fiend in a cloud'). A similar image occurs in the reference to his brother John—'the evil one, In a black cloud making his moan'—in the doggerel sent to Butts in November 1802. Clouds generally symbolize corruption or oppression in Blake, but in 1791–2 a fiend or devil—with the closely related fairies and angels—is likely to have opposite suggestions and to stand for the natural instincts. The principal intention here is perhaps simply to deflate as emphatically as possible the 'simplicity' of *Infant Joy*.

p. 21. NURSE'S SONG (INNOCENCE)

An early version of this song was sung by Mrs. Nannicantipot in *An Island in the Moon*. The possessive in the title may be misleading. This song, unlike its Experience opposite, is not *by* a nurse but *about* a nurse. 15, 16. Blake's spelling of the past participles makes it clear that *leaped* is to be a disyllable and *laughed* (which he spells *laugh'd*) a monosyllable. No doubt he picked up this kind of verbal slovenliness from earlier children's books or the rhymed versions of the Psalms, where archaisms are often used to eke out metre and rhyme. The trisyllabic *echoed* is another example of the same habit.

p. 21. NURSE'S SONG (EXPERIENCE)

2. *Either,* the whispers of the adults in their secretive amours contrast with the happy healthy noisiness of the children; *or,* the older children have already begun to slip away from the eyes of their companions on the green and to exchange amorous whispers in the dale.

4. *green and pale:* still a standard colloquial idiom in Blake's time, the opposite of *hale and hearty*, though he may have been half-remembering 'And wakes it now to look so green and pale' (*Macbeth*, I. vii. 37).

7. To the disillusioned eyes of Experience even the play of children seems futile and unnecessary. There are so many other and more important things children ought to do.

5. *clothing of delight:* Blake is fond of the construction '*of*' *plus abstract noun,* e.g. 'Youth of delight' (*The Voice of the Ancient Bard, l.*1), 'virtues of delight' (*The Divine Image, l.*3), 'the voice of joy' (*Laughing Song, l.*1), 'the forests of the night' (*The Tiger, l.*1). In such phrases the abstract noun should not be regarded as a personification; the meaning intended is equivalent to an adjective, e.g. clothing productive of delight to the wearer, delightful clothing.

18. *called by His name:* a Christian child is called by the name of Christ.

p. 23. THE TIGER

In Blake's symbolic system the larger beasts of prey—particularly lions, tigers and wolves, and their bird-equivalent the eagle—stand for the natural energies. In Innocence such energies need to be tamed (see especially *Night,* p. 40 above), but in Experience their destructive instincts provide a healthy cleansing force. The alternative symbol is fire, a symbol already exploited for the exposition of their mystical metaphysics by the Renaissance alchemists. (Blake admired Paracelsus, though how much he had actually read remains something of a mystery, and he was certainly aware of such alchemical emblem-books as *The Hermetic Museum.*) The unnamed divine artificer's creation of the tiger is an image that combines both symbols. In Blake's mythology the divine blacksmith is Los, the spirit of prophecy, who is often indistinguishable from Blake himself, and there are many parallels between *The Tiger* and the remoulding of Urizen in Los's furnaces in *The Book of Urizen* (1794). *The Book of Los* (engraved 1795) describes the fall of Los through infinite space after his 'Prophetic wrath' has burst the chains in which Urizen, the spirit of mere rationality, had bound him. A further connection with the myths of both Hephaestus and Satan is suggested by the emblem of 'Fire' (a nude warrior with spear and shield, floating with eyes shut in an uprush of enormous flames) in *The Gates of Paradise* (1793)—to which the preliminary sketch in the Rossetti MS. adds 'Forthwith upright he rears from off the pool His mighty stature. Milton.' In the light of these symbolic connections the inspired fifth verse of *The Tiger,* which the Rossetti MS. shows was a later addition, becomes more intelligible. The tiger's creator is not only a God of wrath, the creator of Satan and the French and American Revolutions, but also a God of mercy, the creator of the tiger's 'contrary', the lamb of Innocence.

2. *forests of the night:* forests at night, nocturnal forests (see note on *The Lamb*, *l.*5, above). Rintrah, the symbol of primitive energy, is addressed in similar terms by his mother Enitharmon in *Europe* (engraved 1794), *l.*44: 'O lion Rintrah, raise thy fury from thy forests black!' Night and forests are both oppression-symbols in Blake.

5. *deeps:* perhaps volcanoes rather than oceans.

7. *On what wings:* Blake's fine colour-print known as 'The Elohim Creating Adam' (1795) depicts the creator as a majestic winged human figure hovering in the air immediately above the newly created Adam.

8. *seize the fire:* a reminiscence presumably of the Prometheus legend. Orc, the spirit of revolution, is identified in *The Song of Los* (1795), *l.*21, with the Prometheus of Æschylus's *Prometheus Vinctus*. Blake owned a copy of Robert Potter's very competent translation of Æschylus's tragedies (first edition 1777).

12. *What dread hand? and what dread feet?:* the original draft in the Rossetti MS. shows that 'hand' and 'feet' were at that stage the subjects of a main verb in the next stanza, which then began: 'Could fetch it from the furnace deep.' When this stanza, a much too melodramatic affair, was cancelled the hands and feet were left hanging grammatically in the air. But an appropriate verb is easily understood, e.g. 'wrenched into shape', and Blake's attempt to tidy up the grammar many years later with 'What dread hand forged thy dread feet'—a reading found in one of the engraved copies (now dated *c.* 1802) as well as in the MS. selection from Blake's lyrics seen by Wordsworth *c.* 1803 and by B. H. Malkin not later than 1806—is no improvement because the act of creation now becomes too explicitly a piece of manual labour. Blake dropped the reading in the later copies of *Songs of Innocence and o Experience*.

17-20. *l.*17 is repeated in *The Four Zoas*, Night v. (*c.* 1801), *l.*224 ('The stars threw down their spears and fled naked away'), in a passage that is obviously based on Milton's account of the Fall of the Angels (*Paradise Lost*, Book vi.), the stars being Urizen (Satan) and his associates. Blake's use of the stars to symbolize the Angels is Biblical, e.g. 'When the morning stars sang together, and all the sons of God shouted for joy' (*Job* xxxviii. 7). The stanza can perhaps be paraphrased: After the rebel Angels, weeping with chagrin and distress, had acknowledged their defeat at Christ's hands God created our world, including the animals. It is a proof of His greatness that Christ can be symbolized by both the fiercest and the meekest of the quadrupeds.

In the Rossetti MS. this stanza faces the first draft of the rest of the poem on the opposite page. It has been written over the edge of a swirling sketch of a figure with bent knees and upraised hands who seems to be falling through the air (Satan?). The writing is rather larger and the letters thicker than in the other stanzas—which suggests that it may have been added with another pen and perhaps a day or two later. Some such an interval would explain why both the imagery and the argument detach themselves from those in the rest of the poem. This local detachment adds enormously, of course, to the total range of meaning in *The Tiger*. 19. *Did he smile:* a reference to the formula after each day's creation in the first chapter of *Genesis:* 'and God saw that it was good.'

p. 24. THE BLOSSOM

A poem that has puzzled some commentators. The robin's sobbings need have no allegorical significance. Their principal function in the poem is simply to balance and complement the sparrow's happiness. In the nursery sparrows are traditionally merry ('as happy as a sparrow', and see *Oxford Book of Nursery Rhymes*, p. 133), just as robins are tragic (*ibid.*, pp. 130–3). Blake's point is presumably the unity of vegetable, animal and human nature in Innocence.

p. 24. THE SICK ROSE

In Songs of Experience roses are normally corrupt as well as beautiful, as their thorns and blushes demonstrate. It is significant that *The Sick Rose* is preceded and followed in the Rossetti MS. by two fragments expressing Blake's savagest social criticism. The invisible worm that seduces and destroys the rose is a servant of the 'silent and invisible' Nobodaddy (conventional religion), who is addressed two pages earlier in the MS.:

> Why darkness and obscurity
> In all thy words and laws,
> That none dare eat the fruit but from
> The wily serpent's jaws?

Here the serpent, as often in *Songs of Experience*, symbolizes the clergy, who are able to legitimize love by the marriage ceremony. The worm of *The Sick Rose* amounts to much the same thing, i.e. the corrupting element responsible for the rose's vulnerability is primarily the immorality that permits and encourages loveless marriages. The worm-serpent was also one of Boehme's favourite images, but Blake generally adds a sexual sense to the symbol, and it sometimes stands for the embryo.

p. 25. THE CHIMNEY SWEEPER (INNOCENCE)

Blake was not alone in taking a sympathetic interest in the London 'chimney boys'. David Porter, a benevolent master-sweep of Little Welbeck Street, had recently protested against their exploitation and the appalling conditions under which they worked. An Act of Parliament of 1788, known as Porter's Act, was the first to limit the boys' hours of work and to prohibit their employment until they were eight years old.
2.   According to Porter the sweeps used to pay from two up to eight guineas according to the boys' ages.
6.   The boys' heads were shaved to reduce the risk of their hair catching fire from pockets of smouldering soot.
21.   *we rose in the dark:* it was customary to begin the sweeping at 5 a.m. in the summer and 7 a.m. in the winter.

p. 26. THE CHIMNEY SWEEPER (EXPERIENCE)

The Act of 1788 proved a dead letter, no attempt being made to enforce it. It is clear from the Rossetti MS. that the suffering of the chimney boys typified, as much as anything, the cruelty and callousness of eighteenth-century London. In addition to *ll.*9–10 of his *London* (see p. 56 above) there is a memorable fragment in the Rossetti MS. that may have been intended at one time to form part of *The Chimney Sweeper*:

> There souls of men are bought and sold,
> And milk-fed Infancy for gold;
> And Youth to slaughter-houses led,
> And Beauty, for a bit of bread.

The original draft of *The Chimney Sweeper* in the Rossetti MS. shows that Blake at first intended the second and third verses to form a poem complete in itself, which would then have been about London children generally. By limiting it to the chimney boys Blake greatly increased its effect.
9.   *and dance and sing:* the reference may possibly be to the traditional dances of the London sweeps and milk-maids on May Day, the last of the medieval May Day ceremonies to survive in London.
12.   i.e. 'who construct a false heaven for themselves from the profits they have made out of our misery.'

p. 26. THE LITTLE BOY LOST

An early version of this song is in *An Island in the Moon*, its singer being Quid, who is usually identified with Blake himself.

8. It was a will-o'-the-wisp (the vapour did *not* disappear).

p. 28. A LITTLE BOY LOST

1–4. The logical point the little boy is making was a favourite one with Blake. It is used with considerable acuteness in the early tractates on Natural Religion (*c.* 1788), and it also turns up in a marginal comment on Swedenborg's *Wisdom of Angels concerning Divine Love*, p. 11: 'Man can have no idea of anything greater than Man, as a cup cannot contain more than its capaciousness.'

p. 28. HOLY THURSDAY (INNOCENCE)

Annual services were held in London each Ascension Day, from 1704 to 1877, for the children attending the various London Charity Schools. In 1782 the Charity Schools' Anniversary, as it was called, was transferred to St. Paul's Cathedral because of the increase in the number of children at the Schools. As there is a version of the song in *An Island in the Moon*, which dates from *c.* December 1784, Blake must have witnessed one of the earliest Anniversaries held in St. Paul's.

5. The average attendance was four to five thousand children.

11. *wise guardians of the poor:* not the Poor Law Guardians, but the governors or patrons of the Charity Schools.

p. 30. A DREAM

1. *weave a shade:* i.e. cast a gloom.

3. One of Isaac Watts's *Moral Songs* is *The Ant, or Emmet*.

p. 31. THE ANGEL

In the Rossetti MS. angels symbolize the natural instincts. The cherub who is perched on the shepherd's head in the frontispiece to *Songs of Experience* is clearly symbolic. The little creature's wings are extended, but the shepherd is holding both its arms in his hands—the appropriate treatment for angels or fairies in Experience (see the *Motto to the Songs of Innocence and Experience*, *ll.* 3 and 4). The maiden queen of the dream tried to evade the natural obligations of love in a sentimental affectation of Innocence. It was only when middle-aged that she learnt to accept the necessity of the 'shields and spears' of sex, but by that time it was too late.

The poem is not necessarily the 'contrary' of *A Dream*, though both introduce the words 'a dream' into their first lines, and the 'Angel-guarded bed' of *A Dream*, *l*.2, parallels *The Angel*, *l*.3.

9. *the morn blushed rosy red*: in Blake's symbolic system blushes are always a symptom of sexual corruption.

11-12. Cp. *Day*, a fine Rossetti MS. fragment (perhaps intended to provide a 'contrary' to *Night*), which has much the same symbolism:

> The sun arises in the East,
> Clothed in robes of blood and gold;
> Swords and spears and wrath increased
> All around his bosom rolled,
> Crowned with warlike fires and raging desires.

p. 32. THE DIVINE IMAGE

The essential identity of God and man, one of Blake's central beliefs, was one that he had found in Swedenborg. There is a tradition that this poem was composed in the New Jerusalem Church in Hatton Garden (London), but in 1789 the only Swedenborgian chapel in England was the original meeting-place of the Society in Great Eastcheap. If unfounded the tradition may at least reflect a genuine interest by Swedenborgians in a thoroughly Swedenborgian poem.

p. 33. THE HUMAN IMAGE

This is the poem's title in the Rossetti MS., superseding *The Earth* (cp. *Earth's Answer*). When engraving the poem Blake changed the title to *The Human Abstract*, as if to deny its 'contrary' function. This may have been because he had now written *A Divine Image*, a poem that he engraved but that is not included in any copy of *Songs of Experience* issued by Blake himself. The latter runs as follows:

> Cruelty has a human heart,
> And Jealousy a human face,
> Terror the human form divine,
> And Secrecy the human dress.
>
> The human dress is forgèd iron,
> The human form a fiery forge,
> The human face a furnace sealed,
> The human heart its hungry gorge.

The style and symbolism suggest a date of composition *c.* 1793-4.

15. *the caterpillar and fly:* a symbol for the clergy. Cp. the 55th Proverb of Hell, 'As the caterpillar chooses the fairest leaves to lay her eggs on, so the priest lays his curse on the fairest joys'.

OTHER SONGS OF INNOCENCE

p. 34. LAUGHING SONG

An early MS. version—with the title 'Song 2d by a Young Shepherd' —has survived in a copy of *Poetical Sketches* inscribed 'from Mrs. Flaxman May 15 1784'. In this version the girls with the 'sweet round mouths' are called Edessa, Lyca and Emilie. With the change of their names to Mary, Susan and Emily Blake can be seen recovering the song from the world of pastoral romance, with its exotic latinized names.

p. 35. SPRING

12. *Little girl:* the rhyme with 'small' suggests that Blake pronounced 'girl' *gal*. No doubt, like Keats, he spoke English with what would now be considered a cockney accent.

p. 37. THE LITTLE BLACK BOY

Blake's father is said to have been a Moravian, a small and unimportant Protestant sect in England at that time but one already pre-eminent in the missionary field. *A Song of Liberty,* *l.*12, shows the same sympathetic interest in the negroes' spiritual welfare: 'O African! black African! Go, winged thought, widen his forehead!'
25–6. Almost certainly a reminiscence of a similar passage in Isaac Watts (*Grace Shining and Nature Fainting* in the collection with the general title *Horae Lyricae,* originally published in 1706).

p. 40. NIGHT

11. *moves:* Blake's grammar is often erratic. It would have been a simple matter to emend *l.*9 to 'green field and happy grove'.
17. *thoughtless nest:* there is no *thinking* in Innocence. In *Motto to Songs of Innocence and of Experience* (see p. 112 above) Innocence is distinguished as the condition in which the Good 'think not for themselves'.
27. *thirst:* the thirst of the carnivore for blood.
42. 'The wolf also shall dwell with the lamb, and the leopard shall lie down with the kid; and the calf and the young lion and the fatling together; and a little child shall lead them' (*Isaiah* ix. 7).

OTHER SONGS OF EXPERIENCE AND ASSOCIATED LYRICS
FROM THE ROSSETTI MS.

p. 43. THE LITTLE GIRL LOST

This song and its sequel *The Little Girl Found* were originally included in *Songs of Innocence*, but Blake was evidently conscious of their difference in kind from the other songs and they were transferred to *Songs of Experience* as soon as that series had been prepared. They are really transitional pieces, pointing towards Experience though still falling short of its more completely tragic interpretation of the human condition.
1. *Lyca:* a name that seems to have been invented by Blake. It is also found in the early version of *Laughing Song* (see p. 123 above).

p. 47. THE SCHOOLBOY

Originally included in *Songs of Innocence*; transferred to *Songs o Experience, c.* 1799. Blake distrusted all forms of conventional education. According to Wordsworth's friend Henry Crabb Robinson, who had long talks with Blake in 1825 that he recorded in his diary, he would not 'admit that any education should be attempted except of cultivation of the imagination and fine arts'. The illustration shows what Blake considered the proper occupations of boys of school age—three are playing marbles, four are climbing a luxuriant vine, on top of which another is reading.

p. 48. THE VOICE OF THE ANCIENT BARD

Originally included in *Songs of Innocence*; transferred to *Songs of Experience, c.* 1799. The italic lettering in the engraved text, together with the general difference in tone and subject-matter, suggest that the poem may have been a later addition to *Songs of Innocence*, perhaps in 1790. Its optimistic proclamations may well reflect the extraordinary upsurge of hope that the early phases of the French Revolution created among English intellectuals.

p. 49. 'NEVER SEEK TO TELL THY LOVE'

In a final revision of this song Blake changed 'seek' in *l.*1 to 'pain' and the last line became 'O! was no deny'. Few editors have adopted these disastrous alterations.

4. *Silently, invisibly:* Nobodaddy, the father of jealousy, was also 'silent and invisible' (*To Nobodaddy*, *l.*1; see p. 57 above).

7. *Trembling, cold, in ghastly fears:* in *The Four Zoas*, Night ii., a similar phrase is applied to Urizen's wife Ahania when he left her behind ('Trembling, cold, in jealous fears').

8. *A traveller came by:* Macpherson's Ossianic writings are full of 'travellers' and Blake may have picked up the image there. In his own writings it does not seem to have any consistent symbolic significance.

p. 49. THE CLOD AND THE PEBBLE

A Clod of Clay performs a similar function in *The Book of Thel*, *ll.*85–107. The cynical Pebble may perhaps be considered the realistic 'contrary' of that early and rather sugary Prophetic Book.

8. *metres meet:* the comic jingle underlines the Pebble's cynical realism most effectively. What metres? Meet metres!

p. 53. A POISON TREE

The title is repeated in *The Four Zoas*, Night ii. ('I have planted a false oath in the earth: it has brought forth a poison tree'). The tree was presumably the upas, whose deadly properties had recently been popularized by Erasmus Darwin in *Lives of the Plants* (1789). 'There is just such a tree at Java found' is a cancelled line in *Fayette*, a Rossetti MS. ballad written *c.* November 1792.

p. 54. 'I FEARED THE FURY OF MY WIND'

A variation on the symbolic theme of 'Never seek to tell thy love'.

p. 54. 'WHY SHOULD I CARE FOR THE MEN OF THAMES'

2. *chartered:* in *King Edward the Third*, *l.*9 ('Let Liberty, the chartered right of Englishmen'), Blake had used the word in the sense of 'licensed' or 'privileged', though with a half-reference, no doubt, to Magna Carta as well. Here and in *London*, *ll.*1, 2, there is a clear suggestion the privilege includes licence to oppress. In *The Rights of Man*, pt. 2 (1792), Tom Paine attacked 'charters and corporations' as in effect annulling the rights of the majority of the citizens. Wordsworth discussed with Beaupuy in the spring of 1792 'ancient prejudice and chartered rights' (*The Prelude*, 1805, ix. *l.*329).

1, 2. *chartered:* a repetition of the epithet originally used in 'Why should I care for the men of Thames', an earlier poem in the Rossetti MS. (see p. 125 above). The draft of *London* in the Rossetti MS. has 'dirty street' and 'dirty Thames'.

2. *chartered Thames:* although Blake may not have known it, a statute of 1393 empowered the Lord Mayor to remove weirs, etc., from the Thames, and these powers had been transferred in 1771 to a committee of the Corporation of London.

7. *in every ban:* in every execration or curse (*not* in every prohibition).

8. *the mind-forged manacles:* manacles forged *for* the mind, i.e. to control the mind. The Rossetti MS. shows that Blake began by writing 'The German-forged links', an allusion presumably to George III and his Hanoverian connections.

56. *Every blackening church:* the new London churches built in stone or stucco by Wren and the others soon turned a dirty grey with the enormous increase in the consumption of domestic coal.

12. There is a similar quasi-apocalyptic image in *The French Revolution*, *l.*246: 'And the palace appeared like a cloud driven abroad; blood ran down the ancient pillars.'

15, 16. The images are sometimes interpreted as a reference to venereal disease. But this is to read Blake too literally. The diseases that descend upon the infant and the newly married couple are apocalyptic horrors similar to the blood that runs down the palace walls.

p. 57. TO NOBODADDY

Nobodaddy was Blake's portmanteau nickname for 'Nobody's Daddy'—a contemptuous colloquial 'contrary' to Father of All, the title that the votaries of conventional Protestantism claimed for their tyrannical deity. The name is repeated in some of the later lyrics. God's visibility is one of the central tenets of Blake's special version of Christianity.

p. 57. THE LILY

The lily of the valley and its 'contrary' the thistle were favourite symbols of Boehme's: 'We have a *lily-child* and a *thistle-child* within us.' After his disillusionment with Swedenborg Blake turned more and more to Boehme, whom he found both more congenial and more profound.

p. 60. A LITTLE GIRL LOST

Unlike the preceding Songs of Experience (except the *Introduction*) this poem and *Ah! Sunflower* do not appear in the Rossetti MS., although they are in all the engraved copies. Presumably they were written *after* the Experience group in the notebook. *A Little Girl Lost* was apparently intended as a 'contrary' to *The Little Girl Lost*, before Blake had decided to transfer that poem to *Songs of Experience*. It was probably written in 1793. It is the only Song of Experience addressed to an audience of children—if indeed 'Children of the future age' does not simply mean posterity.

27, 28. A loving look that is terrifying is not really loving, a holy book that terrifies is not really holy. Cp. the hypocritical 'Holy Word' (the Jehovah of Genesis) in the *Introduction* to *Songs of Experience*.

p. 62. AH! SUNFLOWER

4. *Where the traveller's journey is done:* plate 14 of *The Gates of Paradise* has the epigraph, 'The traveller hasteth in the evening'. Plate 13, a pictorial recognition of the immortality of the soul, shows that the traveller's haste is to bring his life on earth to an end, and plate 15 is of Death's Door. As these plates are approximately contemporary with *Ah! Sunflower* the general meaning is likely to be the same. There is a golden world beyond and above the iron world of experience, where the frustrations of sex will no longer make themselves felt.

5. *Where the Youth:* not 'in which' as in *l.*4, but 'to which' as in *l.*8.

p. 62. TO TIRZAH

A poem apparently added *c.* 1800. By 1800 the sin of sins was no longer priestly hypocrisy but materialism; Blake had given up all hope of reform in this world. The Biblical Tirzah was a Canaanitish city that afterwards became Jeroboam's capital. Blake uses it as an antithesis to Jerusalem in the later Prophetic Books, where it is always associated with Rahab (=the materialistic ethics of natural religion or the deists). But, whereas Rahab always connotes sexual licence, Tirzah stands for an unhealthy asceticism or repression of the sexual instincts. The strongly Christian emphasis is confirmed by the quotation in the engraving underneath the text, 'It is raised a spiritual body' (1 *Corinthians* xv. 44).

16. *What have I to do with thee:* 'Woman, what have I to do with thee?' (Christ to his mother at Cana, *John* ii. 4).

THE MARRIAGE OF HEAVEN AND HELL

Like *Songs of Experience*, which it precedes (as far as most of the actual writing is concerned) and overlaps (as far as the engraving can be dated), *The Marriage of Heaven and Hell* is organized round the principle of 'Contrary States'. Its antithetic opposite, however, is not Innocence but Swedenborgianism, the mystical religious system of which Emanuel Swedenborg, the Swedish scientist (but he wrote in Latin), was the founder and prophet. The thirty-three-years-old 'new heaven' to which Blake refers in 'The Argument' alludes to the Last Judgment, or Second Coming of Christ, that Swedenborg saw in one of his visions in 1757, which led to the inauguration of the New Church or New Jerusalem in that year. (Blake added the date '1790' to this passage in Butts's copy.) A good deal of *The Marriage* is the same sort of serious parody of Swedenborg's writings as, e.g. *Nurse's Song* (Experience) is of *Nurse's Song* (Innocence). One of Swedenborg's earliest theosophical works was in fact called *De Coelo et de Inferno*, which was translated into English in 1778 as *Treatise Concerning Heaven and Hell*. A short extract will show how closely Blake's revolutionary 'Argument' follows Swedenborg, while distorting both his theme and his tone of voice. It comes from Swedenborg's sub-section, 'The Equilibrium between Heaven and Hell':

> In order that anything may exist, there must be a universal state of equilibrium. Without equilibrium there is neither action nor reaction; for equilibrium exists between two forces, of which one acts and the other re-acts, and the state of rest resulting from such action and re-action is called equilibrium. . . . All existence, that is, every effect, is produced in equilibrium, and it is produced by active force on the one hand, and passive resistance on the other; . . . spiritual equilibrium or freedom, exists and subsists between good acting on the one part, and evil re-acting on the other; or between evil acting on one part and good re-acting on the other.

Swedenborg's doctrines, according to his own account, were all derived from visionary conversations that he held with angels. In several of his treatises he appends to each chapter a detailed report of one or more of these conversations and the fantastic adventures that sometimes accompanied them in the Angelic Prince's Palace and elsewhere. In the English translations these appear as 'The first Memorable Relation', 'The second Memorable Relation', etc.—a formula that Blake parodies in the five sections of *The Marriage* that are headed 'A Memorable Fancy', in which he records his own much more memorable angelic and diabolic conversations.

Swedenborgianism was still in its infancy in 1790. Although Swedenborg himself had died in 1772, the first public meeting of his English adherents was only held in 1783, when it was attended by exactly five of them. The 'society', as it then called itself, became a separate religious body, with its own place of worship in Great Eastcheap, London, in 1787, and the first general conference of the New Church was held there in April 1789 to determine its essential points of doctrine. Blake was certainly interested and to some extent involved in these developments. His copy of Swedenborg's *Wisdom Of Angels concerning Divine Love and Divine Wisdom* (1788) is heavily and respectfully annotated, and at one point he notes a contradiction between the text and 'what was asserted in the society'. Moreover, in 1789, he and his wife were among the signatories to a minute in the Great Eastcheap minute-book. The disillusionment with Swedenborgianism must have coincided more or less with the disillusionment with Innocence that the poems in the Rossetti MS. record. The marginal comments on Swedenborg's *Wisdom of Angels concerning Divine Providence* (1790) are amusingly and forcibly critical ('Lies and Priestcraft', 'Cursed Folly', etc.). The attractiveness of Swedenborg's system had been the promise it held out of being free from the general corruption of Christianity in the eighteenth century, but a comment like 'that is: till he agrees to the Priests' interest' shows that Blake had now decided that the New Church was no better really than the old. Significantly, it was the taint of predestination that he detected in Swedenborgianism that the marginal notes are most concerned with. The moral basis of Experience is the absolute freedom of the individual will.

The Marriage of Heaven and Hell is more, of course, than a lively satirical refutation of Swedenborgianism. The 'Proverbs of Hell' might almost be called a prose version of *Songs of Experience*. One of the proverbs—'The cut worm forgives the plow'—was originally two lines of a cancelled stanza in the Rossetti MS. of *The Fly*, and there are many links in the symbols both employ (e.g. the identification of lions and tigers with 'wrath') and in the general point of view. Moreover, the success of the 'Proverbs of Hell'—they are decidedly the best thing in *The Marriage*—is due to Blake's ability to utilize and extend a popular form, just as the Songs of Experience derive formally, and perhaps more than formally, from English folk-song. Some stimulus must also be conceded to the *Aphorisms on Man* of Johann Kaspar Lavater, which had been translated by Blake's painter-friend Fuseli in 1788—and which Blake read with passionate interest and concern, to judge by the nature and number of his marginal comments. Lavater was an introspective moralist in the tradition of Pascal and Vauvenargues, and it is interesting to find Blake responding so wholeheartedly to these very un-English aphorisms.

The poems in free verse with which *The Marriage of Heaven and Hell* begins and ends were a first shot at the heavy and chaotic sublimity that is the staple of the later Prophetic Books. If the book was not etched until 1793, as seems possible—the title-page is without a date—the two poems may have been written rather later than the proverbs and the rest of the prose. 'A Song of Liberty' is an abbreviated version of *America* (engraved 1793), though it is in the rhythmical prose of the Authorized Version and not in the loose six-stress line that Blake used and abused in most of his apocalyptic works.

This selection reproduces the text of the first eleven and the last three plates of *The Marriage*. All that has been left out are the last four 'Memorable Fancies'.

Title. 'Good and Evil are here both Good and the two contraries Married' (Blake's marginal comment on Swedenborg's *Divine Love*, *p.* 56).

The Argument. The contrast is between primitive Christianity, when the just man could be meek, and the eighteenth century, when (owing to the corruption of Christianity) humility has become the mark of 'the sneaking serpent' (the time-serving clergy) and the just man must be filled with a righteous, destructive anger.

1. *Rintrah:* an important figure in Blake's mythological system, which was still embryonic at this date; like the Tiger he stands for the natural energies, such as those liberated by the American and French Revolutions.

2. *swag:* an archaic form of *sway*.

p. 65. *This is shown in the Gospel:* John xiv. 16.

p. 66. *How do you know but every bird:* an unconscious reminiscence apparently of Chatterton's

> How dydd I know that ev'ry darte
> That cutte the airie waie
> Myghte nott fynde passage toe my harte
> And close myne eyes for aie?

A Song of Liberty. Modelled on the Song of Deborah and Barak (*Judges* v. 2–31). Many of the phrases are repeated in *America* (1793) and it is clear that the poem is a song of triumph at the success of the American and French Revolutions. The 'new-born terror' is Orc, the Spirit of Revolution, and the fall of the 'jealous King' (=Urizen) in *v.*15 symbolizes the victory of the Americans over European tyranny. This was Orc's appearance in 'the western sea' (*v.*13). The next phase begins with Orc 'in his eastern cloud' (*v.*19, i.e. the French Revolution). Blake's confidence in a similar French victory suggests that he was writing after Valmy (September 20th, 1792), where the French had routed the invading Austrians and their allies.

*v.*3. *France, rend down thy dungeon:* the Bastille fell on July 14th, 1789.

*v.*9. *Flagged:* with their flight impeded by (an archaism).

*v.*16. *Urthona's dens:* Urthona was the symbol of primitive, brutish nature. In the 'Preludium' of *America* Orc is the prisoner of Urthona, but is able to burst the chains of jealousy.

Chorus. *For everything that lives is Holy:* a phrase that sums up Blake's opposition to Protestant asceticism. He uses it in *America, The Four Zoas*, Night ii., and elsewhere.

LATER LYRICS: A SELECTION

The Book of Ahania and *The Book of Los*, the last of the shorter Prophetic Books, were both engraved in 1795. Only one copy survives of each, and they are not included in any of the lists of his works that Blake offered for sale. Presumably he was dissatisfied with them, either on technical grounds—they are not relief-etched like the other Prophetic Books but by the ordinary process of intaglio etching—or as symbolic poetry. The following years were devoted to the composition of *The Four Zoas* (originally called *Vala*), a mythological allegory of formidable length and complexity. But this, too, did not satisfy Blake, even after wholesale revision and recasting, and it was not engraved at all, although passages from it were worked into *Milton* (dated 1804) and *Jerusalem* (also dated 1804, though its engraving cannot have been completed until *c.* 1820). Throughout this 'prophetic' period he wrote next to nothing in rhyme, which he seems to have considered 'the rotten rags of Memory' (*Milton*, f. 42, *l.*41) and below the dignity of the poetry of Inspiration, and the only lyrics he can be said to have *published* are 'And did those feet in ancient time', which follows the prose Preface to *Milton*, the three connected pieces in the interchapters of *Jerusalem* and the cryptic verses added *c.* 1818 to *The Gates of Paradise*.

Of the poems in manuscript only those in what is known as the Pickering MS. (after Basil Montagu Pickering, the publisher, who bought it in 1866) can be considered to have reached an approximately final form. The Pickering poems are usually dated 1801–3, and they may well have been copied out about then,[1] but the absence of all Christian references in most of the poems suggests that many of them were written before Blake's 'conversion' in or about 1800. *The Mental Traveller*, the most remarkable of the poems in the Pickering MS., is probably contemporary with the first version of *The Four Zoas* (1797), with which the symbolism has many affinities. *Auguries of Innocence*, on the other hand, with its strong Christian emphasis, is clearly a later work.

In 1803 or thereabouts Blake began to use the Rossetti MS. again for rough drafts of poems of ballad type, but it was soon laid aside, and it was not until 1808–11 that he started to fill it with epigrams and gnomic verses. It was at this period that most of *The Everlasting Gospel* was written; a fragmentary addition to it, not in the Rossetti MS., may be later.

An important difference between such poems as *The Mental Traveller* and the Songs of Innocence is that they revolve around a Doctrine of Cycles instead of a Doctrine of Contraries. As early as 1792 Blake had begun to explore the symbolism of cyclic recurrence in the prologue to *The Marriage of Heaven and Hell*, and it is more fully developed in *The Book of Urizen* and *The Four Zoas*. In the lyrics the concept appears with little or no mythological covering, but the symbolism—which has been influenced by occultist sources such as the Jewish Cabala, the alchemical writings of Paracelsus and Cornelius Agrippa, and the Protestant mysticism of Boehme—is complex and often obscure. A further source

---

[1] Similar manuscript collections of some of the earlier poems were seen by Wordsworth (who copied out four of them into his Commonplace Book) *c.* 1803 and by B. H. Malkin in or before 1806.

of the imagery is the Druidism of which Blake had now become an enthusiastic devotee. The Renaissance myth of Pythagoras learning his theory of reincarnation from the French and English Druids—to which Milton refers in *Areopagitica*—had grown to enormous dimensions in the eighteenth century in the hands of William Stukeley, Edward Davies and others. It even penetrated into the more scholarly and responsible histories. It was from the British Druids, according to Thomas Carte (*A General History of England*, 1747, i. 61) that 'the Greeks received several of their usages in the worship of their deities, and some of their most important doctrines, as well with regard to religion, as to the sciences'—a conclusion only reached after a long and detailed discussion of all the available evidence. Blake adopted this nonsense enthusiastically, though with variations of his own. The Druids were the source of all knowledge, but unlike Stukeley's Druids, who were benevolent as well as learned, Blake's Druids are cruel and tyrannical, the corrupt descendants of the earlier noble English savages whom he personifies as the giant Albion.

The best commentary on the later poems are Blake's other writings contemporary with them, especially the *Descriptive Catalogue*, with its various offshoots, that he prepared for the ill-fated exhibition of his pictures in 1809.

p. 71. 'AND DID THOSE FEET IN ANCIENT TIME'

A poem that needs to be read in its historical context. Like its two sequels in *Jerusalem* it follows and clinches symbolically a passage of prose commentary—in this case the 'Preface' to *Milton* (1804)—in which Blake had expounded aspects of his general theme in more or less non-mythological language. The three lyrics are semi-mythological, the public allegory of the 'mental fight'—a positive pacifism like that preached by Boehme ('fighting must be the watchword, not with tongue and sword, but with mind and spirit')—merging into the private symbols of Albion (the giant who represents mankind as well as England), Jerusalem (the Holy City that is also Albion's 'Emanation' or spiritual counterpart), and Satan (who symbolizes at this stage in the mythology the human Reason divorced from the Imagination). The Preface is a spirited attack on the 'stolen and perverted writings' of Greece and Rome and their modern imitators, who 'depress mental and prolong corporeal war'. They were 'stolen', of course, because Blake had learnt from the Druidists that Greek and Latin culture derived from that of

Ancient Britain and not *vice versa*, and he is only extending the notion in his apparently jingoist claim that Christianity and true art (Jerusalem) also began in England.

The basic image of the rebuilt Jerusalem had been used in *The Four Zoas*, Night ix., where its achievement precedes the renewal of the 'ancient golden age' (Innocence). The prose address 'To the Christians' (*Jerusalem*, f. 77) explains that 'to labour in knowledge is to build up Jerusalem', the term 'knowledge' including the study or practice of the true 'Art and Science' that emanates from the Imagination. Although the ultimate source of the image is biblical, Blake must have known the great Elizabethan hymn 'Hierusalem, my happy home', which has a similar metre and appears to be echoed once or twice in the *Jerusalem* lyrics. The contrast between the clarity and conviction of 'And did those feet', and its sequels, and the pretentious confusion of the Prophecies in which they occur is one more example of the benefit he derived from writing in an existing popular tradition.

1–8.   The feet of *l*.1 are generally taken to be those of Christ (the 'Lamb of God'), but the logic of the poem's structure—a pattern, similar to that in *London*, of four parallel instances, each two lines long —will not permit this interpretation. The feet are presumably those of Albion who had walked England's mountains in the same period of prelapsarian Innocence when Jerusalem had been built in England. In that case the structural pattern is (i) human (Albion), (ii) divine (Christ), (iii) 'the Countenance Divine' (God), (iv) human (Jerusalem). A similar interpretation has been proposed by Denis Saurat, *Blake and Modern Thought*, 1929, p. 85. The abrupt opening suggests that the original initial stanza may have been cancelled. The Rossetti MS. shows this was a method Blake sometimes used to increase a poem's dramatic intensity.

8.   *dark Satanic mills:* a recurrent symbol in the later Prophecies of the mechanical and merely analytical rationalism that Blake described as 'the state called Satan'. The mills are sometimes water-mills, occasionally windmills, usually handmills worked by slave labour, but the symbolic core is always their 'dark Satanic wheels' (*Jerusalem*, f. 12).

9–12.   Albion's bow is described in *Jerusalem*, f. 97, in similar terms:

And the bow is a male and female, and the quiver of the arrows of love
Are the children of this bow . . .

In Blake the energy symbols are usually *primarily* sexual.

134

From the prose interchapter 'To the Jews', which follows Chapter One of *Jerusalem*. The first few sentences will show what it is all about: 'Jerusalem the Emanation of the Giant Albion! Can it be? Is it a truth that the learned have explored? Was Britain the primitive seat of the patriarchal religion?'

1, 2. In Blake's childhood the open countryside, with farms, fields, hedges and woods, began on the other (northern) side of the 'New Road from Paddington to Islington' (the modern Marylebone Road and Euston Road).

13. *The Jew's-harp House and the Green Man:* the Jew's-harp House, a well-known tavern and tea-garden in what is now Regent's Park, had been the Jew's-harp Farm in Blake's childhood. The Green Man was a wayside inn at the top of Great Portland Street.

14. R. Horwood's *Plan of the Cities of London and Westminster* (1789–94) shows several ponds in what is now the south-east corner of Regent's Park.

15. *Willan's Farm:* a large dairy farm occupying most of the south-west end of Regent's Park. Thomas Willan (*d.* 1818) must have built his farm-house there sometime in Blake's boyhood.

24. *Satan's synagogue:* cp. *Revelations* ii. 9, iii. 9.

25–34. The last public execution at Tyburn was in November 1783. Near to it (approximately the modern Marble Arch) was an ancient stone which is marked on John Roque's map of London (1745) as 'the Stone where Soldiers are shot'. Blake seems to be identifying this stone with 'London Stone', another very old stone near St. Swithin's Church in the City, which Camden, the Elizabethan antiquary, had made famous as the central milestone of Roman Britain. It was only a short next step, for Blake, to superimpose on the Tyburn stone a rôle as the central altar of Druid sacrifice, which in its turn was a relic of the ruins of Atlantean Jerusalem. Hence the description of the parish as 'mournful ever-weeping Paddington'.

37. *Albion's Spectre:* the Spectre or purely reasoning activity is a recurrent term in Blake's later Prophecies. The central theme in *Jerusalem* is Albion's disintegration into a separate Spectre (Satan) and Emanation (Jerusalem) and their final reunion through the intervention of Christ.

41. *Lambeth's Vale:* Blake was living in Lambeth when *The Four Zoas*, the precursor and in part the first version of *Milton* and *Jerusalem*, was

written. Lambeth is south-west of Poplar and Bow, and north-east of Malden.

65–88. The speaker of these lines is clearly Albion.

p. 75. 'ENGLAND! AWAKE! AWAKE! AWAKE!'

From the prose interchapter in *Jerusalem* addressed 'To the Christians'. A similar, if less poetically successful, appeal is made by the 'Vision' of Albion on f. 97 of *Jerusalem*:

> Awake, awake, Jerusalem! O lovely Emanation of Albion,
> Awake and overspread all nations as in ancient time;
> For lo! the night of death is past, and the eternal day
> Appears upon our hills. Awake, Jerusalem, and come away!

The passage is a nice example of the way Blake's style descends into rhetoric, when he speaks in the idiom of the Old Testament, whereas the popular ballad tradition—if only because its lines are short and its rhyme-words generally monosyllabic—keeps him to words in general colloquial use. On the one hand, 'overspread'; on the other, 'felt her feet'.

p. 75. THE GOLDEN NET

Text from the Pickering MS. with minor corrections from the Rossetti MS. The title may come from Edward Young's *Night Thoughts* ('a golden net of Providence', Night ix., *l.*1400), which Blake had recently illustrated. (The first part of the edition, all that was ever published, appeared in the autumn of 1797.) The poem has been alternatively interpreted as the net of chastity or the net of nature interposed between man and reality. The two interpretations perhaps come to the same thing, the illusions of sexual love being characteristic of Vala, the Nature Goddess. The three complementary virgins are clearly related to the threefold maidens of *The Crystal Cabinet* with their beguiling 'threefold smile', and to the threefold vision of 'soft Beulah's night' described in the lines sent to Thomas Butts, November 22nd, 1802. The threefold vision of Beulah (=approximately, romanticism), though superior to twofold vision (=poetic metaphor) and single vision (=direct prose statement), was greatly inferior to the fourfold or prophetic vision.

A difficult poem. The male cycle—baby, youth, husband, old man, lover, baby—seems to symbolize mankind's progress from barbarism to civilization and then, with the decadence of civilization, a return to barbarism. The female cycle—old woman, virgin, baby, maiden, old woman—represents nature's reactions to human progress. The various stages in this conflict of 'contraries' may be taken to symbolize the degrees of human control over, or submission to, nature. In the first stage (male baby-old woman) man is completely at the mercy of nature (he is the aboriginal savage). In the second stage (youth-virgin) he has developed sufficiently to be able to begin the conquest of nature, which has no terrors for him now. In the third stage he is able to exploit nature in a healthy balance of the two contraries, but this is followed by the fourth stage in which nature's powers have been forgotten by man, until it finally revenges itself on a decadent society. And so on. Some of the poem's details are extremely obscure, but if read in this sense Blake's general argument is clear enough. The second half of the cycle is apparently concerned with man as individual and his subjective progress and corruption, whereas the first half diagnozes the relationship between the human group and the external material world.

21-4. An episode described in more detail in the 'Preludium' to *America*. There the youth is Orc, the personification of political revolution, who at the age of fourteen is able to snap the chains in which he is bound and then rape his gaoler's daughter, 'The shadowy daughter of Urthona'.

33-6. Cp. *Riches*, a Rossetti MS. fragment written *c.* 1792:

> The countless gold of a merry heart,
> The rubies and pearls of a loving eye,
> The indolent never can bring to mart,
> Nor the secret hoard up in his treasury.

41. *His grief:* presumably, the products of his painful industry.

p. 80. THE CRYSTAL CABINET

A poem with much the same symbolic content as *The Golden Net* (see the note on p. 136 above). The fragility (unreality) of the state of Beulah (romanticism) causes the disillusioned dupe, who had mistaken its idealistic sentimentality for a philosophy of life, to return to the cyclic conflicts of contraries described in *The Mental Traveller*, which make up this life.

24–8.   Cp. *The Mental Traveller*, especially *ll.*85–6.

p. 81.   AUGURIES OF INNOCENCE

This series of more or less disconnected distiches recalls the 'Proverbs of Hell' in *The Marriage of Heaven and Hell*. The attacks on sceptics and unbelievers suggest *c.* 1800–3 as the probable date of composition. The title may only be intended to refer to *ll.*1–4.

And yet forgives the butcher's knife: cp. 'The cut worm forgives the plough' ('Proverbs of Hell', no. 6).

p. 83.   'MOCK ON, MOCK ON, VOLTAIRE, ROUSSEAU'

These lines from the Rossetti MS. follow an epigram *On the virginity of the Virgin Mary and Johanna Southcott* (who had announced in 1802 that she was about to become the virgin mother of Shiloh, a second Christ). In Blake's earlier writings (*The French Revolution*, *ll.*276–83, and *The Song of Los*, *l.*49) Rousseau and Voltaire are applauded as the prophets of revolution, but with his 'conversion' *c.* 1800 their Deism led him to disown them (cp. *Milton*, f. 24, and *Jerusalem*, f. 52).

p. 83.   MORNING

A Rossetti MS. fragment of *c.* 1803. The poem's meaning is elucidated by a diagram in *Jerusalem*, f. 54, which equates the west with 'Pity' and the east with 'Wrath'. By reversing the sun's progress and proceeding eastwards to the west, i.e. against the direction of nature, the prophetic spirit will be able to allay the conflicts inherent in the evolution of the physical world. The image is expanded and expounded in the blank verse insertion in the interchapter of *Jerusalem* addressed 'To the Christians' (f. 77). (There the fiery wheel of Natural Religion revolves 'From west to east against the current of Creation' and 'Opposing Nature', but Jesus 'Creating Nature from this fiery law' has transformed the wheel into that of a religion of forgiveness.)

p. 84.   *Extracts from* THE EVERLASTING GOSPEL

Transcribed into the Rossetti MS. *c.* 1810. By then every page in the notebook had something on it, so Blake had to tuck the poem into odd corners in short instalments. Even so, separate pieces of paper had also to be used, some of which have been lost, and it is difficult to reconstruct what has survived in the order Blake intended. The title comes from *Revelations* xiv. 6, 'And I saw another angel fly in the midst of heaven, having the everlasting gospel to preach unto them that dwell on the earth, and to every nation, and kindred, and tongue, and people'.

p. 86. TO THE ACCUSER WHO IS THE GOD OF THIS WORLD

An epilogue to the revised edition of *The Gates of Paradise* (*c.* 1818). In its original form (published by Blake himself, May 1793) this curious work professed to be nothing more than a didactic children's book. At that time, except for brief captions under the illustrations, it had no accompanying text. When he re-issued the book years later Blake added some cryptic octosyllabic couplets that were intended to explain the symbolic meanings of the plates, and the title was changed from *For Children The Gates of Paradise* to *For the Sexes: The Gates of Paradise*. A prologue and epilogue were added at the same time. Under the epilogue there is an illustration of a traveller sleeping under a hill, with Satan appearing above him as his dream.

1. *Satan, thou art but a dunce:* echoes the denunciation of Lorenzo in Young's *Night Thoughts* (end of Night the Eighth), 'Satan, thy master, I dare call a dunce'. Blake prepared elaborate illustrations to *Night Thoughts* in 1796–7.

3. In *Jerusalem*, f. 61, the personified Jerusalem hears the voice of Jesus saying: 'Man in the Resurrection changes his sexual garments at will./Every harlot was once a virgin, every criminal an infant love.'

7. The 'Son of Morn' is almost certainly Lucifer.

APHORISMS AND EPIGRAMS

Blake made no attempt to publish any of the gnomic verses or epigrams in the Rossetti MS. It is not even certain that he showed them to friends. The poems that he interlarded with the prose of his letters to the Flaxmans and the Butts are very different in tone. Most of the epigrams must be considered as 'private' as such prose *cris de coeur* in the Rossetti MS. as 'I say I shan't live five years, and if I live one it will be a wonder' (June 1793), or 'Tuesday, January 20, 1807, between two and seven in the evening—despair', or 'I always thought that Jesus Christ was a snubby or I should not have worshipped him, if I had thought he had been one of those long-spindle-nosed rascals' (*c.* 1810).

p. 88.　*Of H——'s birth.*

H—— was William Hayley. Although Blake recognized Hayley's genuine kindness, he found his fussy old-maidish interferences extraordinarily irritating. Byron described his copious verses as 'For ever feeble and for ever tame' (*English Bards and Scotch Reviewers*, l.313).

p. 89.　*A petty sneaking knave.*

Mr. Cr—— was R. H. Cromek, an engraver who had set up as publisher and commissioned Blake to prepare a set of illustrations to Blair's *Grave*. Blake had been promised the engraving of the illustrations as well, but Cromek broke his part of the bargain and employed a rival engraver instead. Another piece of sharp practice in which Cromek was involved was in connection with Blake's fresco of the Canterbury Pilgrims. Cromek had seen a sketch of Blake's picture and then persuaded Thomas Stothard to paint one on the same lines and complete it before Blake's elaborate painting was ready.

INDEX OF TITLES AND FIRST LINES

Rintrah roars, and shakes his fires in the burdened air . . . 63